Crime and Banishment

NUISANCE AND EXCLUSION IN SOCIAL HOUSING

Elizabeth Burney is a Senior Research Associate at the Cambridge University Institute of Criminology. Her early career was as an urban affairs specialist on *The Economist,* when she also sat as a member of the Cullingworth Committee on council house allocation. She has researched and published extensively on race relations and on criminal justice—including books on the magistracy and on youth justice. She is a volunteer with Victim Support.

Crime and Banishment
Nuisance and Exclusion in Social Housing

Published 1999 by
WATERSIDE PRESS
Domum Road
Winchester SO23 9NN
Telephone or Fax 01962 855567
E-mail:watersidepress@compuserve.com

ISBN Paperback 1 872 870 79 1

Cataloguing-in-Publication Data A catalogue record for this book can be obtained from the British Library.

Printing and binding Antony Rowe Ltd, Chippenham.

Crime
and
Banishment

NUISANCE AND EXCLUSION
IN
SOCIAL HOUSING

Elizabeth Burney

Criminal Policy Series: Editor Andrew Rutherford

WATERSIDE PRESS
WINCHESTER

Foreword

Elizabeth Burney has produced a pioneering exploration of the borderland between housing policy and criminal policy. Her study reaches to a paradox at the very heart of the New Labour project in Britain: tackling 'social exclusion' in neighbourhoods, weighed under by multiple deprivation, by methods which carry the markers of exclusion. Burney skillfully traces the strengthening of the powers of local authorities and other social landlords to 'police poor tenants' through housing and other civil legislation over recent years.

To this incisive review of civil powers, Elizabeth Burney adds an equally incisive account of the anti-social behaviour order, introduced by the Crime and Disorder Act 1998 and which took effect in April 1999. This new power, available to the police and local authorities in England and Wales (but not to the police in Scotland) is the most striking example to date of New Labour's *penchant* for 'mixing the best' of the civil and criminal law. She is justified in raising concerns that this quasi-criminal remedy will be mostly used against children and young persons (the minimum age against whom an order may be made is ten in England and Wales, and 16 in Scotland). The author wryly notes the comment of a social housing provider that the good intentions of the Social Exclusion Unit have been pitted against the imperatives of the Crime and Disorder Act.

At the centre of Elizabeth Burney's exposition are tensions arising from competing definitions of 'community'. She leaves the reader with the arresting question: 'What kind of order, then, awaits the people of those neighbourhoods today marked by the blight of deprivation and exclusion?' While she does not attempt a full answer, her analysis points in a direction which is bleak and disturbing.

I am delighted to welcome this timely and thought provoking study of the criminalisation of social policy as a valuable addition to the Waterside Criminal Policy Series.

Andrew Rutherford
Editor
Criminal Policy Series
July 1999

Crime and Banishment
Nuisance and Exclusion in Social Housing

CONTENTS

Acknowledgements

Thanks to a grant from the Nuffield Foundation, the basis for this book was laid during a study tour of troubled housing areas in many parts of Britain. At that time I did not know what I was going to write: I just wanted to look and listen. Many people professionally involved, whether as housing managers, lawyers or policemen were most generous with their time in explaining to me the problems of crime and disorder in their areas and how they were dealing with them. I cannot name them all for obvious reasons but hope that I have given a fair picture of the difficulties they face and that if they read the book they will find the analysis offered helpful. My warmest thanks to them and, also, to the ordinary residents whom I met and whose determination in the face of local troubles was impressive.

I could not have reached so many key people so quickly without introductions, on the housing side, from Rebecca Tunstall of the London School of Economics (who also provided valuable background briefing) and, on the police side, from various senior officers contacted through the Master of Studies course at the Cambridge Institute of Criminology. Further local authority introductions, and a great deal of information, came from Tim Winter of the Social Landlords' Crime and Nuisance Group.

Special thanks to Caroline Hunter and Suzie Scott who briefed me on some of their findings on the use of legal powers by social landlords to deal with 'neighbour nuisance'. Their reports are being respectively carried out on behalf of the Joseph Rowntree Foundation and the Scottish Office.

The Cambridge Institute of Criminology is a wonderful place from which to conduct research touching not only on many aspects of that discipline but also extending into other fields where criminologists are less familiar figures. Printed and human resources are unparalleled, starting with the Radzinowicz Library; and when this was exhausted there was always the University Library, the Squire Law Library and the Land Economy library. Above all I have valued the support and constructive criticism of colleagues, particularly Professor Anthony Bottoms, Jennifer Davies, Janet Foster, and Professor Andrew von Hirsch. Stuart Bridge in another part of the Law Faculty, and at an early stage Alan Holmans in the Department of Land Economy, also gave very valued advice and help.

Beyond Cambridge, meetings with Tim Bell, Sean Damer, Professor David Donnison, Professor Alan Murie, Professor Susan Smith, Jerry White and Jeanette York were all in different ways thought provoking.

Thank you to everybody, especially to those who gave so much time, either in conveying information, taking me round their 'patch', discussing ideas, or taking trouble to go through my draft and making useful suggestions. As ever, any mistakes are mine alone.

Elizabeth Burney
Cambridge Institute of Criminology
March 1999.

Introduction

This book aims to plot the paths by which law and order politics has moved into new ground. The new, and largely unexplored, territory surrounds the development of the landlord-tenant nexus in the social housing sector as a means of suppressing crime and disorder. This has been absorbed directly into the New Labour agenda of populist toughness whilst at the same time apparently offering a blind eye to methods which may clash with another government aim, that of reducing 'social exclusion'. In policies which have sometimes been arrived at almost by accident, the civil law has been seized upon as a tool for disciplining 'anti-social' tenants and nasty neighbours. Housing legislation passed by the Conservative government has introduced new methods, including the power to exclude undesirable people altogether from the social housing sector, which still provides about one fifth of the nation's homes.

In truth, the long-standing processes which tend to concentrate social conflict and crime in some of the most deprived neighbourhoods need to be understood before the uncomfortable manifestations can be reduced. Therefore, I have tried to set the new exclusionary policies in the historical, social and economic context of the 'managed market' of municipal housing. I have also, in the first chapter, set them in the wider landscape of late modern society.

Landlords, both public and private, have always been able to impose rules and standards within the conditions of tenancies, with a view to maintaining the value of property and the peaceful co-existence of residents. These are matters of private, or civil, law which can be recognised as forming part of the web of social order but which have seldom operated overtly in the sphere of crime control. Under the pressures created by changes in the housing and job markets in the late twentieth century, resulting in small areas with very high concentrations of crime and disorder, new approaches have been adopted by social landlords—in particular, a number of local councils within the main conurbations. Backed up by legislation (primarily the Housing Act 1996) rules have been rewritten to facilitate the threat of eviction as a means of crime control and to allow access to council housing to be denied to perceived troublemakers .

This book will seek to place these developments in the context of wider issues of social exclusion and exclusiveness. There is no denying that there are a number of residential areas where extreme social breakdown calls for exceptional measures; the latter moreover can sometimes be shown to have worked. But the existence of such places feeds into much wider public anxieties and suspicions of those whom the

Victorians had no scruples about labelling 'the dangerous classes'—in other words, fear of what the poor might do to the comfortable life-style of the majority. On both sides of the Atlantic for the past 20 years the growing social divide has spawned academic and popular nostrums about the threat of 'disorder' and disorderly people which have fed into policing practice and the management of space by a range of authorities, and been translated in various forms into legislation. The recent rise in Britain of popular censure directed at 'nuisance neighbours' and 'anti-social behaviour' has brought new forms of control to the surroundings of the homes of the poor, and has penetrated family life within the home.

The new methods of controlling household behaviour adopted in Britain in the social housing sector are only a small part of a wider scene. They are worth studying because they provide an illustration of how shifting social and political attitudes can have quite sudden and far-reaching manifestations within legal and administrative structures which control the way that people live.

The first chapter will therefore provide an overview of theories of present-day society which depict fragmented social relations, privatisation of crime control, increased spatial segregation, and control of semi-public space to exclude unwelcome strangers.The use of civil law as crime control is placed in this context. The chapter summarises developments in American thinking about neighbourhood decline and the ways in which these have, and have not, been mirrored in Britain.

The second chapter takes an historical view of landlord-tenant relationships. It outlines the changes in access to social housing, the development of bureaucratic control systems, and past attitudes to 'difficult tenants'. It describes the changing housing market of recent years and the associated social polarisation, and the role played by government and local bureaucracies in the residualisation process. *Chapter 3* explores empirically the nature of crime and disorder in the places where the most deprived groups of people, and their children, cluster within the social housing sector. It highlights some of the difficulties and dilemmas of housing managers in these contexts.

Chapter 4 will look at what lies behind the growing concern with 'nuisance' behaviour, what types of behaviour are involved and what is known about their extent. It charts the politicisation of the concepts of 'neighbour nuisance' and 'anti-social behaviour', and the resulting rush to sometimes inappropriate legislation. *Chapter 5* looks in some detail at the legal and administrative tools now available to social landlords, on whom the burden of keepers of the peace has fallen. The implications of using tenancy enforcement and selective access to waiting lists as a form of crime control include the possibility of further social exclusion.

Chapter 6 takes a closer look at some of the implications of these developments and highlights tensions between prioritising housing need and improving neighbourhood stability; and between granting tenants more power over their own neighbourhoods and housing people who are not welcome to them. The issue of holding parents, as tenants, responsible for their children's behaviour to the extent of eviction is examined. This leads to the question of how far local authority landlords should adopt a policing role, and some possible disadvantages as well as advantages of the statutory police/local authority co-operation of the Crime and Disorder Act 1998. How can we ensure that local priorities help to reduce social exclusion, rather than to enhance it?

The political signals are not altogether encouraging. The Home Secretary, Jack Straw, at the second reading of the then Crime and Disorder Bill on 8 April 1998,[1] told the House of Commons that 'The Bill represents a triumph of community politics over detached metropolitan élites'. As he re-iterated in an article in *The Times* the same day:

> For many years, the concerns of those who lived in areas undermined by crime and disorder were ignored or overlooked by people whose comfortable notions of human behaviour were matched only by their comfortable distance from its worst excesses.

The New Labour party knew better: in contrast to the 1980s, they were no longer captive to single-issue pressure groups, claimed the article. Instead:

> In the period before last year's general election, my colleagues and I spent much of our time talking to those at the sharp end of the problems of crime and disorder—victims, the police, magistrates, local councils.

That these interested parties too might sometimes constitute pressure groups is not acknowledged in the Home Secretary's statement, but nevertheless forms part of the developing picture.

It is indeed true, as also described in Mr Straw's article and by several speakers in the Commons debate, that areas experiencing high levels of crime and disorder are nearly always represented by Labour MPs. The latter could justly claim that the victims who brought their sufferings to constituency surgeries bore the brunt of repeated excesses far beyond those experienced in more affluent areas. The so-called Left-Realism—recognition by the Left that the poor suffer at the hands of other poor—fitted neatly with the mood of 'popular punitivism' appropriated by both main parties. Tony Blair's pre-election promise to be tough on crime's causes as well as on crime itself held out the hope

---

[1] *Hansard*, HOC 8 April 1998, col. 370.

that in this process structural faults would not be ignored. Yet by the time Blair's government introduced its Crime and Disorder Bill the linkage was barely visible. Since then, the introductory work done by the Government's Social Exclusion Unit[2] has demonstrated the multi-causal nature of neighbourhood deprivation; but this body has neither power nor money of its own. Applying the cures will be much harder than repressing the uncomfortable symptoms.

The idea for this book emerged during 1997-98 when I had the benefit of a Nuffield Foundation Small Grant to visit troubled housing neighbourhoods in different parts of the country to observe the traces of crime and disorder and talk about the associated problems from the point of view of, mainly, police and housing managers but also some residents. What I found seemed to recall a much earlier study of access to social housing,[3] while my understanding of the realities of high crime estates drew on nearly 20 years experience of victim support work and other community involvement, most of it close to my former home in Lambeth. I hope therefore that I am not merely a member of a 'metropolitan élite'.

Since coming to the Cambridge Institute of Criminology my appreciation of the value of theoretical approaches to some of the matters raised in this study has increased, but this book is not a theoretical exercise. It was only towards the end of writing that (in a talk by Professor Nicola Lacey), I was reintroduced to Colin Sumner's ideas about social censures. He wrote;

> The sociology of crime and deviance must therefore become a sociology of social censures; their structural roots, institutional forms, discursive and practical meanings, systems and policies of enforcement, hegemonic functions, effects and significance of "offenders", and normative validity.[4]

I realised that, in rather modest terms, this is what my book is about.

---

2 *Bringing Britain Together: A National Strategy for Neighbourhood Renewal: Report by the Social Exclusion Unit* (London, Stationery Office, 1998).
3 Elizabeth Burney, *Housing on Trial* (London, Oxford University Press for Institute of Race Relations, 1967).
4 Colin Sumner, 'Rethinking Deviance', in *Censure, Politics and Criminal Justice*, C Sumner, ed. (Milton Keynes, Open University Press, 1990).

CHAPTER 1

From Disorder to Exclusion

The privatisation of crime control in modern societies is a theme increasingly explored by criminologists. Against a background of rising crime rates—real or perceived—safety has become a commodity, bought by those who can afford it in the form of security guards, electronic surveillance, physical barriers, and control of access to privatised public space such as shopping malls.[1] The state no longer has (if it ever did) a monopoly of public protection. Even the criminal law and the criminal justice system are now acknowledged to have very limited roles in restraining criminal behaviour, especially where social constraints are failing to operate in their support.

As social and economic structures diversify, so it is often claimed, individuals are less dependent on their immediate neighbourhood and other people within it. Traditions and loyalties which formerly played a greater role in social relations are eroded and with them, as Giddens[2] has argued, the sense of whom to trust. The opposite of trust is mistrust, a gift to the security firms and marketers of hardware from CCTV cameras to personal alarms and front door chains. Strangers are viewed with suspicion and living-patterns conspire to make strangers even of close neighbours. In contrast, close family members are often furthest apart in spatial terms; and the intermediate 'buffer zone' of the neighbourhood may be a place empty of social exchange or, in the worst scenario, provide only hostile encounters.[3]

---

1 Anthony Bottoms and Paul Wiles, 'Understanding Crime Prevention in Late Modern Societies' in *Preventing Crime and Disorder: Targeting Strategies and Responsibilities*. T Bennett, ed. (Cambridge, University of Cambridge Institute of Criminology, 1996).

2 Anthony Giddens, *The Consequences of Modernity* (Cambridge, Polity Press, 1990).

3 I am suggesting that the conventional hierarchy of socio-spatial relations, conceptualised by Hunter, and developed by Wikström, as Private, Parochial, and Public, has for many people become void in the middle layer, while 'private' relations may have little connection with the immediate space of the dwelling. Of course, in the poorest neighbourhoods, there is often little connection with the wider 'public' world of citizens either. See Albert Hunter, 'Private, Parochial and Public Social Orders: The Problem of Crime and Incivility in Urban Communities' in G Suttles and M Zald, eds., *The Challenge of Social Control* (Norwood, NJ, Ablex, 1985); Per-Olof Wikström, *Urban Crime, Criminals and Victims: The Swedish Experience in an Anglo-American Comparative Perspective* (New York, Springer Verlag, 1991).

The theory of 'defensible space'[4] argues that people feel safer if their immediate outdoor environment is not easily accessible by strangers. A new generation of urban builders have taken note, and safe design is a selling point. Private housing developments aimed at affluent purchasers cluster behind high ornamental brick walls and closely barred gates. Inner city public housing estates in the course of regeneration now boast similar defences. In these areas elderly and not-so-elderly people may seek the supervised setting of sheltered housing for reasons of protection. The same instinct drives the middle-classes of 'Fortress America'[5] into the gated communities which dominate suburban life in parts of the United States.[6] Here, space, services and security are privatised and households are governed by a barrage of restrictive covenants—characterised in a study of the 'fortress' phenomenon as 'governing by legal contract not social contact' (Blakely/Snyder: 20).

The physical exclusion of people who might pose a threat, or who merely pursue a different lifestyle, is increasingly to be found in city centres and wealthy suburbs of western Europe, including in Britain. Both electronic surveillance and physical barriers guard against unwelcome outsiders. Walls, steel gates, coded locks and CCTV are the physical manifestations of attitudes which are reflected in life-style choices. Middle-class residents in America have been characterised by Baumgartner as functioning successfully without strong local ties— mixing only loosely on a territorial basis, relying on clubs and associations to supplement their social life, and dealing with potential conflict situations by means of avoidance.[7] Nowadays, theorists often regard heterogeneity as a destabilising factor within neighbourhoods.[8] Yet homogeneity may be more widely socially divisive if it contributes to

---

4 Oscar Newman, *Defensible Space: People and Design in the Violent City* (London, Architectural Press, 1972).

5 E J Blakely, and M G Snyder, *Fortress America: Gated Communities in the United States.* (Washington DC, Brookings Institution Press, 1997).

6 Widely different estimates are given for the numbers of people living in these enclosures, depending on definitions (e.g. whether they include sections of cities 'retrogated' by the introduction of street closures). Blakely/Snyder use a low estimate of 8.4 million, which is 3.3 per cent of the 1995 US population. However G S Alexander ('Civic Property', *Social and Legal Studies* 6.2, 1997, 217-234) puts the figure at 30 million, nearly 15 per cent of the population.

7 M P Baumgartner, 'Social Control in Suburbia' in *Towards a General Theory of Social Control*, vol.2, D Black, ed. (Orlando, Flo., Academic Press, 1984).

8 Robert Bursik, 'Social Disorganization and Theories of Crime and Delinquency: Problems and Prospects', *Criminology* 26, (1998), 519-551. Ethnographic studies in ethnically diverse areas tend to bear out this view: see Sally Merry, *Urban Danger: Life in a Neighbourhood of Strangers* (Philadelphia, Temple University Press, 1981).

suspicion of outsiders and fear of 'difference'. Mistrusted strangers attract the available contemporary stereotypes: for instance, today it is thought necessary as a matter of policy to teach young children that *any* stranger may be a danger.

But what if the aim is to protect the locality from internal threat, in the form of crime or anti-social behaviour by people who have a right to be there? The stranger you fear may also be your neighbour, or your neighbour's son and his friends. Informal ways of dealing with unpopular behaviour within a neighbourhood are less frequently available than in the past. New systems have to be employed and new reliance on administrative and formal solutions has emerged. This includes the recognition that tenants have a right to be heard. So it is no surprise that tenants in poor neighbourhoods are not only increasingly regulated by social landlords, but that they themselves expect a management response to their demands for protection.

Under the category of privatised protection, it is therefore appropriate to subsume what might be called 'legal hardware'. Increasingly, the weaponry of civil, rather than criminal, law is being used in the arena where property rights converge with issues of public protection and control of crime and disorder. Contractual obligations and injunctions can be a way of 'designing out crime' alongside other environmental safety devices.[9] This is clearly to be seen in new patterns of control of tenant households which have developed in the social housing sector, which in turn must be set in the context of the enhanced role of local government as a key player in matters of public safety and social control. It is on these developments that this book will focus.

Paradoxically these safeguards have been introduced at least partly because of the need to counteract the effects of multiple deprivation now spoken of as 'social exclusion'. In other words, part of the rescue package for poor, crime-ridden neighbourhoods is defined in terms of rules which in certain ways mirror the 'government by contract' culture of the exclusive American fortresses. Enforcement of the rules can lead to the exclusion or expulsion of 'anti-social' individuals, thereby rendering the neighbourhood more 'includable' in mainstream society.

Traditionally, tenant householders sign up to certain routine obligations and formal prohibitions, such as not playing music at late hours or using premises for 'immoral purposes'. Respect for neighbours and for the character of the neighbourhood is implicit in these arrangements. What is different in the contracts now widely imposed on the tenants of local councils and housing associations is that new rules are explicitly aimed at control of crime and disorder, and more likely to

---

9 See Lorraine Green Mazerolle and Jan Roehl, eds.,'Civil Remedies and Crime Prevention', *Crime Prevention Studies*, vol. 9 (Monsey, NY, 1998).

be enforced. The new-style rules apply not only in respect of activities within the property, but may extend over the whole neighbourhood. For reasons explained in later chapters, social housing has become increasingly associated with crime and uncivil behaviour, while informal social controls are seen as having weakened. Formal control, expressed ultimately in the threat of eviction for non-compliance, has been deliberately introduced to fill the gap. Crimes committed by council tenants or their children may now carry ancillary penalties restricting their housing rights and freedom of movement imposed via the property rights of their landlord (*Chapter 5*), who is thus capable of punishing through the civil law in ways which may be more onerous than the sentence of the court.[10]

At national level, the perception that certain types of people need to be controlled in new ways has led to increased complexity and confusion at the civil/criminal law interface. This is not only in the specific context of landlord/tenant relations but in the recent 'law and order' legislation by both Conservative and Labour governments. The Criminal Justice and Public Order Act 1994, the Protection from Harrassment Act 1997 and the Crime and Disorder Act 1998 are the main statutes concerned. In different ways these measures are aimed at controlling behaviour by individuals or groups which previously might not have been deemed sufficiently threatening to justify laws which, among other things, stretch definitions of motivation and proof. New curbs have been introduced on new classes of behaviour—harassment, anti-social behaviour—which may or may not be treated as crimes. The law of trespass has been changed to create a criminal offence from what was formerly a private matter. In the opposite direction, civil remedies are increasingly applied (in the example of social housing) to matters which would clearly merit criminal prosecution. To understand how this has come about—and indeed why such innovations seem to be popular politicially—we need first to return to the broader changes in social attitudes and experience indicated in the opening paragraphs.

Visions of (in)security

One can speculate, as other writers have done,[11] as to why a public sense of *local* insecurity has become politicised and, symbiotically, continually

---

10 For a discussion of the principle involved, see Andrew von Hirsch and Martin Wasik, 'Civil Disqualification Attending Conviction: A Suggested Conceptual Framework', *Cambridge Law Journal*, 56(3), November 1997, 599-626.

11 For an overview of the media influence on perceptions of crime, see Robert Reiner, 'Media Made Criminality' in *The Oxford Handbook of Criminology*, 2nd edition, M Maguire, R Morgan and R Reiner, eds. (Oxford, Oxford University

represented in newspapers and on television screens. 'The emphasis is on crime as the product of free-floating evil, diverting attention from any links to social structure or culture'.[12] In so far as they influence public opinion and even raise anxiety, the media themselves form part of the scene in terms of forming the public perceptions which in turn create political pressure to 'do something' about successive sources of threat to our safety. Yet this process must answer some sort of need. Is it that our fragmented society has to reinvent 'community' based on the idea of self-defence against the threat of crime?[13] The hypothesis of Lacey and Zedner, that 'appeals to community are most likely to flourish where the structures of community are most fragile'[14] well expresses the anxiety underlying the use of this mantra, combined perhaps with nostalgia for Britain's brief period of so-called 'post-war consensus'. Defensiveness is also encouraged by the modern tendency of government to shift reponsibility for crime prevention on to individuals, businesses, and local structures.[15]

Recognition of possible political and psychological pressures does not rule out acknowledging the truth of much, and more, of the experience to which public anxiety relates. The demand for control of specific types of crime and disorder in specific contexts usually has a basis in fact, and it could be argued that, if anything, governments and other agencies were slow to recognise the depth of local concerns over matters which did not necessarily rate high on the official crime control agenda. Programmes like 'Safer Cities' tended to rely on police definitions of crime and were not required to seek the views of the local population.[16] Crime rates were not going to be reduced by paying attention to litter, noisy parties, and boys playing football in the wrong

---

Press, 1997). For a local analysis of media influence and gossip on images of race and crime in part of Birmingham, see Susan Smith, 'News and the Dissemination of Fear' in *Geography, the Media and Popular Culture*, J Burgess and J Gold, eds. (Beckenham, Croom Helm, 1985). For crime perceptions in a prosperous Manchester suburb see Ian Taylor, 'Private Homes and Public Others', *British Journal of Criminology*, vol. 35.2, Spring 1995, 263-285.

12 Reiner, op. cit.

13 I have tried to avoid use of the word 'community' wherever possible, but it is sometimes unavoidable as shorthand for 'people defined by the area in which they live' or alternatively 'people with a sense of shared local identity'.

14 Nicola Lacey and Lucia Zedner, 'Community in German Criminal Justice: A Significant Absence?', *Social and Legal Studies* vol. 7 no. 1, March 1998, 7-25.

15 Adam Crawford, *The Local Governance of Crime: Appeals to Community and Partnerships* (Oxford, Clarendon Press, 1997).

16 Adam Crawford, *Crime Prevention and Community Safety: Politics, Policies and Practice* (Harlow, Addison Wesley Longman, 1998), 55.

place. 'Hidden' violence in the home or against minority groups usually claimed less official recognition than burglary and car crime.

In 1990 there were not many local councils who regarded public safety as part of their overall remit. In that year the report of a working group on crime reduction set up by the Association of Metropolitan Authorities[17] discussed how to set about providing for 'local solutions which need to be designed to reflect local variations and conditions' and which, to gain credibility, must 'be broadly defined to reflect those elements *whether legally 'criminal' or not* [author's italics] which the public is prepared to take action to prevent' (p.9 of that work).

In the following year the Home Office Standing Conference on Crime Prevention set the future agenda in a seminal report which argued that any meaningful structure for crime prevention must relate to the local democratic structure.[18] The report was shelved for a while by a Conservative government with no love for local democracy. But for Labour, the views of local councillors in their own high-crime heartlands helped to shape official policy.

'Local solutions' to problems defined by 'public' priorities—however expressed—are key elements in the now statutory local crime and disorder strategies. During the 1990s, in their capacity as social landlords and environmental guardians, local authorities rehearsed versions of this theme through legal enforcement of civil rules—rules which had essentially evolved to protect public health and property rather than in response to democratic demands. Central government began to develop corresponding statutory procedures in order to facilite control of 'nuisance' behaviour. Excising, excluding and banning came to be seen as essential responses to the kind of troubles which sorely plagued some of the poorest in the land. Blaming individual troublemakers proved not nearly as difficult as curing the conditions which produced them.

Local differences matter

A response to crime and disorder geared to 'local variations' must be the right aim but it also has to be proportionate. There are indeed some neighbourhoods terrorised by drug barons, some streets where no unprotected building is safe from burglary and vandalisation, and some public spaces dominated by intimidating gangs. These images may skew popular perceptions in other, safer, residential areas. If people feel insecure for other reasons—for instance through worsening conditions in

---

17 *Crime Reduction: A Framework for the Nineties?* (London, Association of Metropolitan Authorities, 1990).

18 James Morgan, *Safer Communities: The Local Delivery of Crime Prevention through the Partnership Approach* , Standing Conference on Crime Prevention (London, Home Office, 1991).

the job or housing market—they may react with more hostility towards other, 'disorderly', people. Somehow these tendencies have to be recognised and dealt with at the same time as allowing people more say in how their own neighbourhoods are controlled.

Surveys show that for most types of crime and disorder both incidence and perpetrators are highly localised. A minority of the population experiences a concentration of both property and personal crime, especially the latter.[19] As has been shown from the British Crime Survey, if areas are grouped according to their crime rate, those areas in the highest (tenth) decile experience twice as much property crime as the ninth, or next-worst, decile, and three times the amount of violence. Indeed the majority of all violent attacks happen in these top ten per cent of locations.[20] Property crime, in particular, is closely related to the domicile of the offenders—who tend to live close to each other and mostly do not stray far from home to commit thefts, burglaries and damage.[21]

Even within top-crime areas, the number of individual victims is smaller than the overall incidence would suggest. In other words, repeat victimisation is commonplace, so that the unfortunate few are bearing the brunt of crimes. In keeping with this finding, localised studies have shown that neighbourhoods suffering unusual amounts of crime, disorder and nuisance do not experience them in similar fashion all over. In one corner litter, in another rowdy youths, in yet another drug dealing will be the main complaint. Different ends of the same street may produce problems requiring different solutions.[22]

All these things are only partially related to fear of crime, which is much more generalised. As one might expect, anxiety about particular sorts of crime is related to experience, direct and vicarious, and also to personal feelings of vulnerability, though not necessarily in proportion to risk.[23] The measurement of 'fear of crime' is problematic;[24] a lot

19 Graham Farrell, 'Multiple Victimisation: Its Extent and Significance', *International Review of Victimology*, 1992, 85-102; Hazel Genn, 'Multiple Victimisation' in *Victims of Crime: A New Deal*, Mike Maguire and John Pointing, eds. (Milton Keynes, Open University Press, 1988).

20 Tim Hope 'Communities, Crime and Inequality in England and Wales' in T Bennett, ed. op. cit. (1996).

21 For an explanation of the areal measurement of offence rates, offender rates, and victimisation rates see Anthony Bottoms, 'Environmental Criminology' in Maguire, Morgan and Reiner, eds. op.cit. There is however some difference in the various studies as to how far burglars travel.

22 Joanna Shapland, 'Targeted Crime Reduction: The Needs of Local Groups' in T Bennett, ed. op. cit.

23 Michael Hough, *Anxiety About Crime: Findings from the 1994 British Crime Survey*, Home Office Research Study 147 (London, Home Office, 1995).

depends on how the question is posed. What we can say for certain is that the public has a very high general awareness of crime and that crime gets far greater attention in the British media than in comparable European countries.[25] This feeds directly into political priorities and the need for all parties to be seen to pursue policies of crime control.

To sum up so far:

- The geographical incidence of crime and disorder is far more concentrated than the public sense of anxiety about them, which is widely diffused.

- In the high crime areas with concentrations of personal and property crime, there are a small number of people who are repeatedly victimised.

- Public awareness of crime and disorder, and the political response, tends to be fuelled by worst cases.

- Perceptions of the failure of criminal law to prevent neighbourhood crime and disorder have led to increasing reliance on the mechanism of private law.

BROKEN WINDOWS AND BAD BOYS

What, then, are the characteristics of these high crime areas,[26] and how did they get to be the way they are? We shall look at some in more detail in *Chapter 3*. Here we will first examine some of the theories which have developed around the phenomenon, many of them emanating from the United States of America where urban decay has gone further, for longer, than in Britain.

---

24 Stephen Farrall, Jon Bannister, Jason Ditton and Elizabeth Gilchrist, 'Questioning the Measurement of the "Fear of Crime": Findings from a Major Methodological Study', *British Journal of Criminology*, vol. 37 no.4, Autumn 1997, 658-679.

25 For example Lucia Zedner found that, in Germany, 'the mass of traditional crimes which so preoccupy in Britain draw comparatively little media coverage. Crime-related stories occupy much less space in press, radio and television reporting and, as a consequence, attract less political attention and fewer resources'. 'In Pursuit of Law and Order: Comparing Law and Order Discourse in Britain and Germany', *Social and Legal Studies*, vol. 7 no.1, March 1998, 522.

26 This discussion is about residential areas. Many other crime concentrations occur in leisure, transport, commercial and workplace settings.

Although most commentators are broadly in agreement about the ingredients of the problem, they differ in emphasis. Some—most famously James Q Wilson—place responsibility firmly down on the ground, seeing the failure to contain minor disorder as the direct cause of neighbourhood decline. He has little patience with broader socio-economic problems as an explanation. Others like his namesake William J Wilson[27] prefer to raise structural failures, notably the flight of jobs from the inner city, as the root causes of the social afflictions of the inner city ghettos, including crime and disorder.

James Q Wilson and George Kelling, in their colourful essay 'Broken Windows',[28] set out an analysis and an agenda which have been very influential on both sides of the Atlantic, as much in terms of their political as their practical appeal. They argued that minor acts of vandalism and disorder, unless promptly dealt with, create an atmosphere of fear, with multiple types of incivility increasing as people stop caring or daring to do anything to prevent them. 'A stable neighbourhood of families who care for their homes, mind each others' children, and confidently frown on unwanted intruders can change, in a few years, or even a few months, to an inhospitable and frightening jungle' . They believe that '. . . serious street crime flourishes in areas in which disorderly behaviour goes unchecked'.

Their remedy is to clean up graffiti and litter as soon as they appear; mend windows; and above all use police powers to clamp down on uncivil behaviour and even on people who may be doing nothing wrong but whose presence raises anxiety among respectable citizenry.

> Not violent people, nor, necessarily, criminals, but disreputable or obstreperous or unpredictable people: panhandlers, drunks, addicts, rowdy teenagers, prostitutes, loiterers, the mentally disturbed.

The essay is primarily a demand for what is now called 'zero tolerance policing', as a means of re-establishing and reinforcing informal methods of social control. The authors recognise that there is a problem in this. 'How do we ensure . . . that the police do not become the agents of neighbourhood bigotry?' But they do not have an answer, other than relying on better police training. It is a question that has to be raised afresh, in Britain, now that under the Crime and Disorder Act 1988 (for many good reasons) police and local people are supposed to work closely together defining local problems and devising ways of dealing

---

27 William J Wilson, *The Truly Disadvantaged: The Inner City, the Underclass and Public Policy* (Chicago, University of Chicago Press, 1987).

28 James Q Wilson and George Kelling, 'Broken Windows: The Police and Neighbourhood Safety', *The Atlantic Monthly*, March 1982, 29-37.

with them, and have new powers to help them deal with troublesome people.

Wilson and Kelling's scenario has no room for differing sensibilities to the 'incivilities' which they describe, or the differing power of different communities to deal with such things and resist the downward slide.[29] Matthews, reviewing the evidence, argues that 'if we are to take into account the social impact of crime and incivilities, then it is on the poorest and least resourced neighbourhoods that we should focus our attention, rather than on those which are described as "tipping into crime"'.[30] This has, of course, indeed been the focus of much of the estate regeneration action in Britain. But other things have to change as well for the effect to be sustained. A review of some ten years'-worth of initiatives to combat housing-related crime on estates in England and Wales came up with the inevitable: although environmental conditions can be improved, communities will always be vulnerable to crime as long as they remain in poor socio-economic conditions.[31]

A review of the processes of neighbourhood change by Wesley Skogan[32] came to similar conclusions as Wilson and Kelling as to the immediate symptoms. But he, like W J Wilson, described the overwhelming structural force of the flight of economic activity to the suburbs and the 'hollowing out' of the inner city, where only poor, jobless, ethnic minority families remain. Deindustrialisation and the decline of unskilled jobs in Britain have had different geographical and racial patterns in comparison with the United States. But the consequences in relation to the housing market have been comparable, once allowance has been made for the differences created by a much larger public sector element.

A paradigm of the stages whereby the ability of the local community to regulate itself is diminished by crime and disorder is presented by

---

29 Roger Matthews, 'Replacing "Broken Windows": Crime, Incivilities and Urban Change', in *Issues in Realist Criminology*, R Matthews and J Young, eds. (London, Sage, 1992).

30 Ibid, 34. This view is confirmed by research in Stockholm, showing that people in social housing suffer more from various types of disorder, and that there are also significant differences between different estates. Per-Olof Wikström, 'Urban Neighbourhoods, Victimisation and Fear of Crime', in *Changes in Society, Crime and Criminal Justice*, vol 1: *Crime and Insecurity in the City*, C Fijnaut *et al*, eds. (Antwerp, Kluwer Law International, 1995).

31 Steve Osborn, 'Reflections on the Effectiveness of Estate Improvement Programmes', in T Bennett ed. op. cit.

32 Wesley Skogan, 'Fear of Crime and Neighbourhood Change' in *Communities and Crime: Crime and Justice, A Review of Research*, vol. 8, A J Reiss and M Tonry, eds. (Chicago, Chicago University Press, 1986). See also by the same author, *Disorder and Decline* (New York, The Free Press, 1990).

Skogan. As visible conditions decline, causing fear to increase, residents withdraw physically and psychologically from community life. There follows a weakening of the informal processes of social control, especially control of children's behaviour. There is a parallel decline in the organizational and mobilising capacity of the neighbourhood. Business conditions deteriorate, shops close. Delinquency and deviant behaviour increase, both on the part of local youths and from disorderly people coming in from the outside. Everyone who is able to move out does so, and the population who remain consist increasingly of the poorest: elderly people, women and children households, and single jobless men.

This scenario is mirrored in many impoverished and blighted residential areas of Britain. But in some key respects Skogan's North American account does not fit British experience. In particular, it can be argued (*Chapter 3*), that the weakening of economic and social structures in many neighbourhoods of public housing preceded the onset of problematic disorder, although subsequently each exacerbated the other. This can most clearly be seen in the metropolitan areas where pockets of extreme housing market weakness mirror industrial collapse. Moreover the location of criminal areas has strong associations with the workings of central housing policy and local practices, which are formative, and sometimes destabilising, influences in the whole housing market.[33] As Chicago sociologists observed 60 years ago, where conditions are conducive to residential instability, this in turn is closely related to disorder and fear of crime, and these then have the effect of further destabilisation.[34] If one was to pick one key variable in the link between housing and crime, household turnover would be the best bet. And it is the struggle to achieve stable communities which helps to explain the tougher legal line now being taken by local housing managers.

It is most important to recognise that not all poor communities with high crime rates feel the same to people living there. Local differences show up sharply in ethnographical studies, demonstrating that the stereotype of 'social disorganization' does not necessarily follow indices of disorder. The element of self-help and solidarity may actually be quite

---

33 Anthony Bottoms and Paul Wiles, 'Housing Markets and Residential Community Crime Careers: A Case Study from Sheffield' in *Crime, Policing and Place*, D Evans, N Fyfe and D Herbert, eds. (London, Routledge, 1992); Alan Murie, 'Linking Housing Changes to Crime', *Social Policy and Administration*, vol.31 no.5, December 1997, 22-36; E J Reade, 'Residential Decay, Household Movement and Class Structure', *Policy and Politics*, vol.10 no.1, 1982, 27-45.

34 Robert Bursik, 'Ecological Stability and the Dynamics of Delinquency', in Reiss and Tonry, eds. op. cit.

strong; for example a close look at the Meadowell estate on Tyneside, regarded as a typical 'sink' estate, found well-established social and financial support mechanisms which the people valued highly.[35] Even when crime and disorder seems to be overpowering, at a local level grassroots leaders (usually, a few determined women) can still influence the quality of life. Beatrix Campbell's[36] classic exploration of some of the estates which in the early 1990s were shaken by explosions of disorder from jobless youths vividly describes the bitter struggle by some local women to preserve what was left of community. Successful regeneration of 'sink' council estates has always built upon, and facilitated, the will-power of tenants themselves in shaping the future of the area.

The experience of estates such as those portrayed by Beatrix Campbell is detailed in another chapter. On a more theoretical level, the elements necessary for a community to 'tip' into high levels of crime and delinquency have recently come in for further analysis, combining individual and environmental factors. On the environmental side, decline both in the wider infrastructure and in social interaction at the local level help to erode the mechanisms which sustain normative values. This in turn reduces the natural degree of 'guardianship' of public space. Moreoever paid guardians such as caretakers have often been withdrawn. This factor of 'guardianship' is a key element in opportunity-based theories of criminality—unguarded spaces and buildings present more temptations to criminals and less likelihood of apprehension.[37] On the individual side, it is the presence of disproportionate numbers of people who are most likely to succumb to the temptations of crime which raises the likelihood of criminal opportunities being seized upon. The established paradigm of such a person is someone with low self-control and weak ties to conventional sources of socialisation such as school or work. The most persistent offenders are above all characterised by family backgrounds where parenting is inappropriate or inconsistent.[38]

A core of persistent offenders, so the argument goes, in an area of easy criminal opportunities, will attract a wider circle of easily-tempted youths who might not become delinquent if they lived in a less

---

35 Michael Barke and Guy Turnbull, *Meadowell: The Biography of an 'Estate with Problems'* (Aldershot, Avebury, 1992).
36 Beatrice Campbell, *Goliath: Britain's Dangerous Places* (London, Methuen, 1993).
37 Marcus Felson, *Crime and Everyday Life* (London, Pine Forge Press, 1993).
38 David Farrington, 'Human Development and Criminal Careers' in Maguire, Morgan and Reiner, eds. op. cit.; R Sampson and J Laub, *Crime in the Making: Pathways and Turning Points Through Life* (Cambridge Mass., Havard University Press, 1993).

crimogenic area.[39] This can be expressed in terms of mathematical formulae derived from epidemiology.[40] Some people will always be immune, but those who have the propensity to catch the 'plague'—delinquency—will be infected according to their degree of exposure to carriers. The theory is recognised in practice by youth-focussed social schemes which are a standard part of the armoury of area regeneration. In particular, such schemes are intended to divert the young people who are not deeply embedded in crime but who might become so if left at large with their peer group.

YOUTH AS MENACE

Fear of youths, even of children, as potential sources of 'trouble' and danger is a theme which runs through countless studies of people's attitudes to their neighbourhoods. It is part of a recurrent theme of disorderly youth as a menace to respectable society.[41] It is also inextricably tied to wider anxieties about a perceived youth crime wave (although there is no statistical evidence to support this). There is no doubt that young people have always been responsible for a great deal of theft and damage to property, usually petty but occasionally very serious. (The same could be said about the many crimes perpetrated against the young). There is a large literature on the social construction of punitive attitudes to young people and how these attitudes are reflected in current penal policy, which there is no need to go into here.[42] There is also much discussion about changing social mores such as the loss of deference and respect for authority. Complaints that children rudely reject reprimands for misbehaviour from adults in their neighbourhood are no doubt well-founded, as are many of the stories about misbehaviour in schools having become significantly worse.

Where demographic and social forces have created neighbourhoods with disproportionate numbers of children and teenagers, these are often also the poorest residential areas. Some of these, inevitably, will conform to the pattern of high delinquency described above; they will also tend to be messy. They will certainly have a visible youth presence 'hanging

---

39 Per-Olof Wikström, 'Communities and Crime', in *The Oxford Handbook of Crime and Punishment*, M Tonry ed. (Oxford, Oxford University Press, 1998). This essay provides a reasoned overview of theoretical approaches.

40 Paul Ormerod, 'Stopping Crime Spreading', *New Economy*, vol. 4, no.2, 1997, 83-88.

41 Geoffrey Pearson, *Hooligan: A History of Respectable Fears* (London, Macmillan, 1983).

42 For a summary see Sheila Brown, *Understanding Youth and Crime* (Buckingham, Open University Press, 1998).

about', a phrase which carries pejorative overtones even if, in the same breath, the observer remarks that there is nothing else for them to do.[43] 'Hanging about' late at night is especially frowned upon, and for some passers-by a source of unease and fear. Where younger children are involved, disapproval and unease mingles with fears for their safety— hence the provision for 'child curfews' among the new panoply of controls in the Crime and Disorder Act 1998.

The validity of the above generalisations begins to fragment once real places are observed on the ground. Not everybody feels menaced by their local youth, not even the residents of some very 'delinquent' areas. Sandra Walklate's study[44] of two areas of Salford is an important lesson in contrasting attitudes. She defines the difference in terms of trust. One area, mainly consisting of older owner-occupied houses, was undergoing the effects of a declining market and rising crime. Residents felt their safety was also declining, and there was a marked lack of trust between generations. 'We've reached the stage where we suspect all children' was how one elderly lady expressed it. A policeman remarked: 'These people have no trust of even their own sons'.

The contrast with a nearby area, mainly consisting of a large council estate with a very bad reputation in the outside world and a history of crime and vandalism, was very marked. Despite its reputation the people of the area were much more ready to trust each other; their mistrust was largely directed at agents of the state whose intervention was often unwelcome. People knew the youths who formed the local gang but to an extent felt protected by them rather than menaced. Misdeeds could be 'sorted' by appropriate members of the community and the police were relatively seldom called in. In the eyes of the police, the main characteristic of the area was as a source of predators on the external society, particularly in the form of robberies from car drivers stuck in slow traffic.[45]

These two areas, only two miles apart, therefore conform to totally different patterns. The first, with its loss of trust, conforms to a Giddens-

---

43 Ian Loader, Evi Girling and Richard Sparks, 'Narratives of Decline: Youth, Disorder and Community in an English Middletown', *British Journal of Criminology*, vol.38 no.3, Summer 1998, 388-403.

44 K Evans, P Fraser and S Walklate, 'Whom Can You Trust? The Politics of "Grassing" on an Inner City Housing Estate', *The Sociological Review*, vol.44(3), 1996, 361-380; Sandra Walklate, '"No More Excuses!": Young People, Victims and Making Amends', *Policy Studies*, vol.19 no.3/4, 1998, 213-222; Sandra Walklate and Karen Evans, 'Zero Tolerance or Community Tolerance? Police and Community Talk about Crime in High Crime Areas', *Crime Prevention and Community Safety*, vol. 1 no.1, 1999, 11-24.

45 Author's own research.

like stereotype of late modern society. The disorganization caused by crime and the lack of built-in protective mechanisms meant that the residents were very reliant on the police and would have wished them to be more pro-active on the streets. The second area, which probably saw at least as much 'bad' behaviour, preferred to keep the police at arms-length, and certainly did not fit any 'late modern' stereotype of social relations.

Janet Foster's ethnographic study[46] of an East London housing estate paints a similar picture, although one underlying difference was a much smaller teenage population. The area was ugly and shabby and had a very bad reputation in the eyes of outsiders, including officials who were responsible for the estate. But the atmosphere was supportive and neighbours 'looked out' for each other. Even though many long-established residents were well-known for quite serious crime, they were seldom a source of fear, largely because they were familiar as individuals. When anti-social acts were committed, informal methods of dealing with perpetrators were preferred and people were not afraid to challenge bad behaviour. Although an initial survey had shown that people worried a lot about vandalism, car crime and mugging, the ethnographical research found that crime was not really in the forefront of people's anxieties. They were aware of local incidents, but their chief concerns focussed on unemployment and housing problems.

In the course of the study, there were local conflicts which emerged, including cases of racial harrassment. The tenants' association believed that their own way of resolving the issue was preferable to the formal method favoured by the local authority, and fairer than the penalty of eviction imposed through the housing department. But in fact when changes in administration meant that the formal system was no longer working effectively, the study noted that informal sanctions also became less effective in containing crime. Foster concludes that formal structures are needed to back up the natural controls present in a community.

It would be instructive to make an equally detailed study of some of those residential areas which have become publicised through the presence of families accused of wreaking havoc in their own communities. A few notorious case histories have provided political fodder for legislation described in more detail in later pages of this book. Their neighbours, it appears, were united against the troublemakers. Where this happens, local solidarity (or the appearance of it) takes an exclusive form, in contrast to the inclusive relationship with local delinquents described in the Salford example. Presumably much depends on the nature of the behaviour objected to, but other factors

46 Janet Foster 'Informal Social Control and Community Crime Prevention', *British Journal of Criminology*, vol. 35 No. 4, Autumn 1995, 563-583.

such as the length of association with the area may also be important. Complex histories of feuding families sometimes loom in the background, such as were observed in Bottoms *et al's* study of Sheffield estates.[47]

Hope and Pitts[48] refer to school enmities being pursued in post-adolescent life on some estates. Baumgartner[49] identifies the presence of support groups—youthful bands of friends, or extended families for example—as a factor encouraging 'aggressive prosecution of grievances'. She argues that working class neighbourhoods are more likely to feature these networks, so that conflict is not avoided to the extent that it is in middle class areas. This observation rings true, but the odds are not always well balanced. Not everyone in the same area is able to mobilise aggressive support, and those without protection may be easily victimised by those who do have it. There is sometimes a very fine line between 'informal social control' and bullying. Without knowing the full situation it is always risky to pass judgement on local conflicts. Devising policies to deal with the many versions of community disruption and deviance is even more difficult.

EXCLUSION AND EXPULSION

At a time when 'social exclusion' has become a catchword and a national concern, the experience of many people to whom that term might apply is therefore of increasing physical exclusion. Formal exclusion from school increased more than fourfold in just four years, 1990/1991 to 1994/1995.[50] The increased exclusion of individuals from access to social housing or to certain areas within it is described in detail in a later chapter. The Criminal Justice and Public Order Act of 1994 made trespass a criminal offence and made it much easier to expel gypsies and other travellers from open ground. It also relieved local authorities of the duty of providing official sites. There are many places, such as city centre pubs, where people of unkempt or workstained appearance are unwelcome, however well behaved. In America, the sequel to 'broken

---

47 Anthony Bottoms, Ray Mawby and Polii Xanthos, 'A Tale of Two Estates' in *Crime and the City: Essays in Memory of John Barron Mays,* David Downes, ed. (Basingstoke, Macmillan, 1989).

48 John Pitts and Tim Hope, 'The Local Politics of Inclusion: The State and Community Safety', Social Policy and Administration, vol.31 no.5, December 1997.

49 Baumgartner op. cit.

50 Department of Education and Employment, *More Willingly to School: An Independent Evaluation of the Truancy and Disaffected Pupils GEST Programme* (London, DofEE, 1995).

windows' was the purging of homeless people from the streets and subways of New York.[51] Thousands of people every year are forbidden access to private shopping malls in Britain lest they disturb the bland atmosphere which characterises these enclaves. 'Defended locales' observe Bottoms and Wiles[52] 'necessarily involve excluding those that are seen as dangerous and undesirable, and the more such tactics are used to serve only private interests the more crude such exclusions may become'.

The mechanism for these exclusions is the law of property which permits the private owner to dictate who may or may not enter the area. As ever more segments of cities come under commercial or institutional private ownership, freedom of movement and opportunity is curtailed. A case[53] which raises grave concerns was that of a group of mainly black youths in Wellingborough, Northamptonshire, who were banned for life from the central shopping mall where they had been meeting, even though no wrongdoing had been proven. This meant that not only could they not use the main shopping facility of the town but would never be able to get employment there either.

Public landlords who use exclusionary private law do so in the name of the greater good for the greater number of their tenants. But, like any other property owner, preserving the marketability of their assets is also their concern. Exclusion in the general housing market has usually worked simply through the price mechanism, plus any informal systems operated by gatekeepers such as estate agents and building societies, although landowners have also been able to stipulate restrictions. Council landlords, the next chapter will show, have in the past used administrative means to manipulate access by different types of tenant to different quality housing estates. It could be said that today's more legalistic methods of exclusion of undesirable tenants, exercised by social landlords of all kinds, at least have the merit of greater openness and are therefore potentially more open to challenge.

It is significant that, as with city centre developments, this involves more regulation of semi-public space. Landlord sanctions are increasingly applied to behaviour in 'the space between'—the roads, car

51 George Kelling and Catherine Coles, *Fixing Broken Windows: Restoring Order and Reducing Crime in Our Communities* (New York, The Free Press, 1996).

52 Anthony Bottoms and Paul Wiles, 'Crime and Insecurity in the City', in C Fijnaut *et al*, eds. op. cit.,1.36.

53 *CIN Properties v Rawlins* [1995] 2 E.G.L.R. 130. See *The Observer*, 26 May 1996 and Kevin Gray and Susan Francis Gray, 'Civil Rights, Civil Wrongs, and Quasi-public Space', *European Human Rights Law Review*, 1999, Issue 1, 46-102. The case was appealed before the European Commission on Human Rights but no intervention by the Commission was possible because Britain had not ratified the relevant part of the Convention on Human Rights.

parks, shopping precincts etc that lie outside the tenanted properties themselves. These, of course, are the locations where disorder and crime are likely to be located and where people may feel most fearful.

But local authorities are no longer the only players. Increasingly tenants themselves—often as means of strengthening disordered communities—are gaining a measure of control over the way their neighbourhood is managed, and tenant leaders are often the toughest in demanding enforcement of rules and punishment of rule-breakers.[54] Housing associations and co-operatives have been acquiring council stock, and increasingly authorities are divesting themselves of residential property altogether. And under the Crime and Disorder Act 1998, everybody in a neighbourhood, whatever their housing tenure, may be consulted on the formation of the new, local, 'crime and disorder strategies' which are now a statutory duty for police and local councils to operate together. The likelihood of tension between potentially exclusive strategies and the goal of social inclusiveness is plain—to take only one example, the imposition of curfews on all children in selected areas. As Adam Crawford has pertinently remarked, '. . . lines need to be drawn between forms of identity and difference which foster tolerance and democracy and those which undermine them'.[55] This will not be easy when, both socially and historically, other lines are etched into many places which tend to perpetuate divisions and conflicts. The yearning for local tranquillity readily fosters demands for exclusion and expulsion— of whom, and where to?

In this process, the aims and practices of local managers, and wider influences affecting the housing market, will have an important, perhaps decisive, influence. So deeply has the present been shaped by past priorities, that the next chapter will be devoted to the history of how housing of the poor has evolved through the twentieth century.

---

54 Anne Power, *Estates on the Edge: The Social Consequences of Mass Housing in Northern Europe* (Basingstoke, Macmillan, 1997). This study found similar trends across 20 estates in five different countries.

55 Crawford, op. cit., 307.

CHAPTER 2

Decent Houses for Decent People

Octavia Hill, the founder of social housing management, was a star witness to the Royal Commission on Housing of the Working Classes of 1884.[1] She told the inquiry how she bought and managed houses with sitting occupants of a kind who would never be tolerated by the companies whose business was building working class housing. She took on drunkards, criminals and above all what she described as 'the destructive classes', against whom no appliance or fixture was safe. They seem to have exercised even greater ingenuity in this respect than the 'pram in the rubbish chute' tenants of today. According to her:

> Drains may be more or less easily got at and they must be able to throw boots down them, and crinolines, and bonnets and house flannels and the drains will get stopped up; and the taps will be wrenched off and baluster rails burnt.[2]

In her opinion the numbers of such people in London was 'a very large part' of the population but 'the criminal class is not so very large'. Her solution—her famous trademark 'system'—relied on rigorous control and surveillance of behaviour: 'I know nothing for them but some individual power and watchfulness', she told the commissioners. Through close personal contact and what she called moral training, combined with a carrot and stick method whereby money saved on repairing 'destruction' would be spent on improvements, she claimed to instill less anti-social habits. She admitted:

> It is a tremendous despotism, but it is exercised with a view to bringing out the powers of the people, and treating them as responsible for themselves within certain limits.[3]

---

1 *Parliamentary Papers*, 1884-5, XXX.
2 Octavia Hill was called to give evidence on 9 May 1884 and her evidence is to be found in pp.208-308.
3 Octavia Hill is someone who arouses strong positive and negative feelings even today. Whilst Anne Power, for example, admires her personal, small-scale aproach to housing management (*Property Before People*, London, Allen and Unwin, 1987), for some any good she did is outweighed by her intrusive bossiness. Sean Damer describes her as 'this revolting person' (*From Moorepark to Wine Alley: The Rise and Fall of a Glasgow Housing Scheme*, Edinburgh, University of Edinburgh Press, 1989, 37).

Octavia Hill's 'system' did not appeal to the providers of 'model dwellings' for the working classes, such as the Peabody Trust. Peabody and other such companies were very selective in their choice of tenants (as indeed Miss Hill was when choosing new tenants), since regular rent paying, sanitary habits and good behaviour were paramount.[4] These were reinforced by strict regulations which, among other things, reflected the contemporary fear of disease. (Tenants had to agree to all family members being vaccinated and being removed to hospital in any case of infectious disease). Other rules governed the duty and timing of cleaning common parts, the places where children must not play, forbad the running of a shop or sub-letting, or keeping dogs, and made tenants responsible for damage to fixtures in their rooms. 'Disorderly and intemperate tenants will receive immediate notice to quit'. And, of course, no rent arrears were permitted.[5]

Such rules were intended to impose discipline, to a degree which many found irksome, and which matched the barrack-like architecture of the model dwellings. Like many of the regulations imposed by Victorian property owners, they were designed to limit access to the right class of person. Similar rules were later adopted by municipal landlords, who were just as anxious to secure quiet, responsible tenants who were reliable rent payers.

Two versions of social landlordism were therefore on offer at the end of the Victorian era: inclusive (on conditions), and exclusive. The first, which few except Miss Hill espoused, meant taking people as you found them but then insisting that they learn to conform to a minimum standard of respect for property and the discipline of regular rent-paying. She described this as self-help but at the same time recognised it as 'a tremendous despotism'. Peabody and the like had a different version of benevolent despotism, tempered by the need for a standard return on their investment. This imposed a high entry standard which had the effect of excluding anybody unable to meet it. In both cases, household behaviour was directly or indirectly controlled by the landlord to a significant degree.

The two methods—control of access, and control of tenants' conduct and housekeeping standards—have both been practised widely by council landlords for the greater part of their existence. The perceived need to promote and preserve good standards and regular rent paying came to dominate housing management. 'Standards' meant more than just keeping a neat home. The idea implied the preservation of a sanitised zone—council housing—protected from the dangerous

4 A S Wohl, *The Eternal Slum: Housing and Social Policy in Victorian London* (London, E Arnold, 1977).

5 A S Wohl, pp.159-60, reproduces the full Peabody regulations.

infections and social threats of the slums. Municipal housing in its early years represented public *safety*.

Fundamentally, the nation's health—moral as well as physical—was believed to be at stake. Housing policy had evolved as an almost panic response to the twin evils of overcrowding and disease which appeared to be destroying the nation from below, bringing the threat of crime and disorder as well as pestilence and 'degeneracy'.[6] It was therefore, for the first half of this century, firmly in the hands of the powerful medical officers of health. David Garland[7] has described the medicalisation of social and penal policy and the consequential focus on methods of categorising individuals within pre-ordained terms of reference. Housing has not generally been viewed within this frame, although the underlying problem of poverty, and the resulting mismatch between rent levels and wage levels, required careful scrutiny of new tenants.[8] As Anne Power[9] has shown, tenants' needs took second place to rent collection and property management in the expanding public sector. People had to be fitted to property, and would-be tenants were often classified accordingly. But slum clearance meant taking on some people who might not otherwise have been viewed as suitable tenants. Hence local authorities had to respond to the problem of housing those whom Octavia Hill would have called the destructive classes, or in Victorian parlance, 'the undeserving poor'.

Municipalities were usually able to match 'best' and 'worst' tenants to appropriate property in the market conditions which prevailed until late in the twentieth century. Until the practice was discouraged, many had systems for grading tenants according to their housekeeping standards. Usually they were able to insist on neat homes and well-tended gardens. (The *moral* as well as practical value of the family vegetable patch was a feature which interwove the early council estates with the garden city vision) .

This chapter will argue that a dramatic shift in the housing market and changes in the terms of access to social housing have left social landlords in the post-industrial era with more poor and problematic

6 For an anthology of contemporary descriptions of slums and their inhabitants, see Peter Keating, *Into Unknown England, 1886-1913* (Manchester, Manchester University Press, 1976).

7 David Garland, *Punishment and Welfare* (Aldershot, Gower, 1985).

8 A very interesting local study of how tenants of different economic and social status, and different housekeeping standards, were dealt with, is to be found in Robert Ryder 'Council House Building in County Durham, 1900-39' in *Councillors and Tenants: Local Authority Housing in England and Wales, 1919-39*, M Daunton, ed. (Leicester, Leicester University Press, 1984).

9 Anne Power (1987), op.cit.

tenants and fewer of the traditional means of supporting or controlling them. Later chapters will show how, in the struggle to regain their own territory, they have made a large investment in security hardware and turned to both civil and criminal law enforcement as a management tool.

'Incapable of a standard of decency'

With hindsight it therefore seems ironic that municipalities might never have become major players in the housing market had it not been for the fear of revolution. Rent strikes and industrial unrest before and during the First World War led to the highly controversial imposition of rent controls in 1915. But this was not in any way a solution to the acute housing shortage, aggravated by wartime building restrictions. By 1919 the plight of ex-soldiers and their families threatened to boil over into open revolt. Clydeside had already led the way in the pre-war rent strikes, and again became the scene of violent confrontations in which police were backed up by army tanks. Even the Home Counties saw events such as the burning of Luton Town Hall at a (cancelled) victory celebration which assumed threatening connotations in the face of contemporary events in Russia. Amid the slogan 'Homes Fit for Heroes' the Addison Act of 1919 placed a duty on local councils in areas of shortage to build houses with the help of a central government subsidy. In a summing up speech at the Bill's second reading, Major Astor, Parliamentary Secretary to the Local Government Board, declared: 'The money we propose to spend on housing is an insurance against Bolshevism and revolution'[10]

The burst of housebuilding which followed was short-lived, but it provided some attractive, high quality cottage-and-garden style estates, modelled on the garden-city ideal. Old-style terrace housing was associated with the unhealthy crowded conditions which were blamed for the poor physique of army recruits, and worse. 'Bad housing' said Major Astor, ' is a very real factor in the production of immorality. The way to assist our fallen sister is not to provide her with rescue homes but with a decent, clean, healthy home in which she can live'.[11]

The new-style estates were, however, too expensive for most of those who might be driven by poverty into deviant occupations. It was the skilled workers who had led the protests and demonstrations against high rents and housing shortages and it was they who alone could afford the products of the Addison Act. The old terrace houses remained as the homes for the unskilled, low wage sector of the population, who were left largely unaffected by municipal building programmes until the slum clearance drive of the 1930s. Private rents remained on average far lower

---

10 *Hansard,* 7 April 1919, col. 1956.
11 Ibid, col. 1949.

than council house rents well into the second half of the twentieth century.[12]

The association of overcrowded slum housing with unhealthy, immoral and criminal populations of low intelligence had become deeply entrenched during the late Victorian period, the inhabitants seen as almost a race apart. Slum housing was one of the stages upon which positivist roles and nature/nurture debates were played out. An admittedly extreme example was a view mooted—though not openly espoused—by the Inter-Departmental Committee on Physical Deterioration, which reported in 1903:[13]

> It may be necessary, in order to complete the work of clearing overcrowded slums, for the State, acting in conjunction with the Local Authority, to take charge of the lives of those who, from whatever cause, are incapable of a standard of decency which it imposes. In the last resort this might take the form of labour colonies on the lines of the Salvation Army Colony at Hadleigh, with powers, however, of compulsory detention. The children of persons so treated might be lodged temporarily in nurseries or boarded out. With a view to enforcement of parental responsibility, the object would be to make the parent a debtor to society on account of the child, with the liability, in default of his providing the cost of a suitable maintenance, of being placed in a Labour establishment under State supervison until the debt is worked off.

This passage makes somewhat chilling reading in the context of the anti-social behaviour orders, child protection orders, and parental responsibility orders being introduced 95 years later: a roll-call of individualised remedies severed from any structural connections. Its real significance however lies in the assumption that there is some kind of duty, shared between central and local government, 'to take charge of the lives of those who . . . are incapable of a standard of decency which [the State] imposes'. It was a huge extension of the private, benevolent-minded, interference of the Octavia Hill 'system'. It is not conceivable that it would ever have been carried out to the degree suggested. But local authorities were to find themselves 'taking charge of lives' in the same spirit. As the century progressed, and the rehousing of slum dwellers could not be avoided, the belief that they were 'incapable of a standard of decency' was one which pervaded policy, and influenced practice, although there were always those who fought against it.

---

12 J B Cullingworth, *English Housing Trends, Occasional Papers on Social Administration, Number 13* (London, G Bell and Sons, 1965). See below p.46.

13 *Report of the Interdepartmental Committee on Physical Deterioration*, 1903, vol 1, cited in J M Mackintosh, *Trends of Opinion about Public Health, 1901-51* (Oxford, Oxford University Press, 1953).

Divisions of opinion surfaced in the Parliamentary debate, in April 1930, on an important Bill providing subsidies for slum clearance. Arthur Greenwood, Labour Minister of Health, emphasised that slum dwellers were an ordinary cross section of the public. He cited in support the experience in Hull and Wakefield, where medical officers of health had been agreeably surprised. The Wakefield MoH had said: 'We were warned that tenants turned out of slum houses would soon make slums of municipal houses . . . [instead] the people are responding wonderfully to their new and better environment'.[14] But not all medical officers were so sympathetic. Lt-Colonel Freemantle, a past President of the Society of Medical Officers of Health and now an MP, evoked heated rebuttals when he claimed that people lived in slums because of faulty heredity and social failure.[15]

John Wheatley, the outspoken Glasgow MP who had himself, as a Minister, been responsible for key legislation on council housebuilding, denounced the way that :

> When we are dealing with the slum-dweller, we always deal with him as if he were an inferior type of humanity . . . [We] treat them as we treat the Crown colonies, as a section of humanity not fit for self-government, but to be taken by their superiors and coaxed and led to that higher plane where they may be allowed to run loose for themselves. That mentality governs this House, even though it may be subconscious.[16]

Many writings of the period confirm the existence of prejudice against slum dwellers, expressed in crude stereotyping by supposedly expert commentators.[17] Extreme even for its day (1935) was the book *Slums and Slummers* by the public health inspector for Whitstable, C R A Martin (whose authority rested on a textbook about food hygeine which remained a standard work for decades). 'An appreciable percentage of the occupants of the slums', he wrote, '. . . are born slum-makers; a curse to any landlord, private or muncipal . . . This vicious class may be considered the core of the whole slum problem. It consists of people of varying degrees of viciousness: drunkards, hooligans and loafing idlers down to the hardened criminals and moral degenerates'. A few years later, in wartime, members of the genteel classes who received into their homes mothers and children evacuated from urban slums were shocked at the lack of personal hygiene and toilet training, and tended to attribute

---

14 *Hansard,* 7 April 1930, cols. 1801-1802.

15 Ibid, col. 1911.

16 Ibid, col. 2016.

17 Jim Yelling, 'The Metropolitan Slum' in *Slums,* M Gaskell, ed. (Leicester, Leicester University Press, 1990).

such things to social and moral deficiencies rather than simply the effects of living without running water or modern sanitation.[18]

Wartime evacuation nevertheless aroused the nation's conscience and rehousing people from the slums that remained after the blitz was adopted with determination along with post-war reconstruction. From now on municipal authorities moved into the role of major providers of working class housing. Having regard also to the need to approximate rent levels more closely to income levels, the estates built to house tenants decanted from slum clearance and 'decrowding' orders tended to be of lower standard than the rest.[19] The rehousing obligation was limited to families and excluded many other households, such as owner-occupiers, and single men. But among those families were some who did not adapt readily to the constraints of a municipal tenancy. Hence the categorisation 'problem family', i.e. people whom social workers and housing managers saw as the cause of difficulties to themselves as professionals. In a process which has been acutely analysed by Sean Damer,[20] the pathologising of 'problem families' went hand in hand with that of 'problem estates'—whole neighbourhoods viewed as unsatisfactory, even threatening, on account of the poverty and perceived fecklessness of the residents.

'Problem families' were people whose social and, often, intellectual deficiencies were thought to render them incapable of running a decent home; they became objects of close supervision, mainly in terms of hygiene, care of the property and, of course, rent paying capability. By extension, slum dwellers moving into council homes were often closely supervised until they had proved themselves.[21] Extreme cases were the 'undesirable tenants' who were not acceptable in conventional council property. 'How shall the undesirables be dealt with?' asked a 1938 report by the Central Housing Advisory Committee (CHAC), who were considering the management of slum clearance tenants on council estates. Part of the answer, it believed, was close supervision. The bad cases should be dispersed among 'families of a good type' where they might learn by example. The committee rejected the Dutch solution of compulsory segregation in separate communities. But it warned against the special risk of putting bad tenants into flats, where:

---

18 *Our Towns* (Oxford, Hygiene Group of Women's Group for Public Welfare, 1943).
19 Anne Power (1987), op.cit.
20 Sean Damer, op. cit.
21 Sean Damer describes the rigorous visiting routine of Glasgow's 'Green Ladies', the uniformed housing / health officers.

The impact of one antagonistic person on another, the quarrels of children, the behaviour of a noisy tenant, may be magnified out of proportion to the actual event and cause a general feeling of unrest and dissatisfaction.[22]

The proportion of tenants who might need continuous supervision was considered to be only five per cent—a figure reflected in later estimates, including present-day surveys of 'nuisance' neighbours.[23]

After the Housing Act 1935 local authorities were obliged when choosing tenants to give priority to large families and those living in overcrowded or insanitary conditions. These were bound to include a proportion in the 'problem' categories. Concern on this score grew in the post-war era of large-scale council building and resettlement of people from old slum neighbourhoods onto suburban estates. The subject was further aired in CHAC report of 1955, entitled *Unsatisfactory Tenants*,[24] following an inquiry among a cross-section of 101 housing authorities.

To avoid the problem of defining an 'unsatisfactory' tenant, councils were only asked to provide figures about families whose behaviour resulted in a notice to quit—an estimated 0.1 per cent of all 2.5 million council tenants. Owing rent was by far the commonest reason for eviction; next, neglect of house or garden; third and last, 'behaviour causing a nuisance to neighbours'. The latter covered 'a variety of behaviour likely to disturb or annoy neighbours, such as lack of control over children, quarrelsomeness and abusive language'. But this category did not feature as a major concern and the report had no specific recommendations about it. Almost the whole discussion was about containing rent arrears; the need to avoid eviction if at all possible by means of close management and family support; and on how to prevent families breaking up if they did have to be evicted. The 'treatment' ethic was, as with other social ills of the time, seen to be the answer: 'the authority should not regard eviction merely as a solution of their difficulties, but as a stage in the treatment of a family' was the committee's advice. The value of family casework was emphasised and, also in keeping with the times, child welfare featured strongly in the thinking of the report.

---

22 Central Housing Advisory Committee, *The Management of Municipal Housing Estates*: First Report of the Housing Management Sub-Committee (London, HMSO, 1938).

23 See for example the 1998 NACRO report, *Nuisance and Anti-Social Behaviour: A Report of a Survey of Local Authority Housing Departments*, which found that authorities in England and Wales had to respond to complaints about three per cent to seven per cent of their tenants in one year. See below p.111.

24 Central Housing Advisory Committee, *Unsatisfactory Tenants: Sixth Report of the Housing Management Sub-committee* (London, HMSO, 1955).

The question of whether to segregate 'unsatisfactory tenants' was revisited, and rejected, but provision of alternative older property, poorer and cheaper, was seen as a reasonable solution. It is clear that the unsatisfactoriness of the tenants concerned related (as with Octavia Hill's 'destructive classes') very largely to their treatment of property and very little to their treatment of other people.

Responses from individual local authorities show that many had resolved the question of what to do with unsatisfactory tenants by keeping them off their estates altogether and housing them in a variety of makeshift ways. Some were swopped with more acceptable private sector tenants; others put in specially purchased sub-standard terraced housing or war-time pre-fabs; Nissen huts on disused airfields and requisitioned army camps were used where available.[25] The conclusion drawn in the report was that, while local authorities had a duty to house families whose standards made them unacceptable to other landlords, in order to do so they would need to utilise sub-standard housing and provide social skills training.

More detail emerged about the kind of people viewed as 'unsatisfactory'. Most were the familiar 'problem family'—non-copers in every sense, with unruly children, quarrelsome with each other and neighbours, likely to be in trouble with the law. If housed on estates, only a few of such tenants could quickly make life a misery for the rest. Rehabilitation in 'half-way houses' run by social services was sometimes attempted. Billericay in Essex gave a detailed account of their experimental scheme for housing a small group of families in prefabs where they received intensive intervention from all relevant services, in the hope that they could eventually become mainstream tenants.

> The families in question appeared to have no responsibility whatsoever either in moral or social conduct. Parents and children were frequently in court for a variety of offences. The younger children were seriously neglected and in general their living conditions were deplorable . . . in any financial dealings with the council the record was bad .

Only one responding council, Hampstead, made a further distinction between (1) 'dirty tenants'—who could not look after house or children and were a serious nuisance to neighbours, and (2) 'anti-social tenants'. The latter:

> . . . keep their accounts clear and their home in a clean condition. They may indulge however in drunkeness and brawls and exercise no control over their children. The children are destructive on the housing estate and terrorise other children . . . both children and parents may be insolent and

---

25 PRO ref: HLG 37 (Written responses from the sample authorities).

abusive to other tenants and to the council caretakers . . . sometimes [they have] a criminal record which causes great apprehension among neighbours.

This seems to be the exception that proves the rule—tenants who were violent and aggressive but without housekeeping problems must have been an insignificant number within the already small minority of 'unsatisfactory' tenants.

'Unsatisfactory' tenants were not going to go away and remained a permanent item on the management agenda. But Popplestone's 1979 survey in six local authorities concluded they were often victims rather than the cause of the problem, or at any rate scapegoats for unsuitable housing situations.[26] (Twenty years ago, structural as opposed to individual interpretations had a readier audience than in more recent times).

> Behind complaints about neighbouring tenants often lie a host of other grievances that have not been dealt with. They often stem from the lack of choice available to council tenants over the question of who to live next to. People with similar life styles and outlooks are likely to get on better with people who share these outlooks, than people who live radically differently. Also tenants are often obliged to live in housing patently inadequate for their needs. . . . We came across complaints which stemmed from the stressful conditions brought about by physical densities as well as the high child population on some estates. . . . Families living at very high densities cannot be expected to tolerate disruptive families . . . Unsatisfactory tenants are the scapegoats for intolerable conditions.

It is interesting to note that this 1979 survey makes no explicit connection between 'difficult tenants' and crime, even though at this time 'safety' on estates was beginning to become a concern.[27] Vandalism was a constant preoccupation, inside and outside houses, but rarely a matter for the police. Racism was rearing its head. Some councils reported attacks on caretakers. These things were recognised as management problems but more in the sense of endemic behaviour to be merely contained. Popplestone considered the housing manager's position to be an impossible one, as 'the guardian of that ideal world in which all tenants maintain the standards of behaviour envisaged in the Housing Acts and codified in tenancy agreements'. He concludes: '. . . it is arguable that the

---

26 Gerry Popplestone and Chris Paris, *Managing Difficult Tenants*, Centre for Environmental Studies Research Series, 30 (London, CES, 1979).
27 For example the Greater London Council funded NACRO's 'Safe Neighbourhood Unit' from 1980.

burden of responsibility placed on housing management is in fact the main problem'. Has recent history proved him right?

'How to Keep Clean and Win a Council House'

This was the title of a chapter in a book published in 1967[28] which analysed access to public sector housing from the point of view of ethnic minorities (known in those days as 'coloured immigrants'). By then exclusionary practices had burgeoned. It was common for local authorities to operate allocation schemes which effectively excluded—or consigned to their worse properties—anyone who did not fit the stereotype of the conventional family (assumed to be white) of two married parents, with not too many children, who were able to show they kept a clean home and a 'clean' rent book (i.e. one with no record of arrears). The belief evinced in the 1955 report that even 'difficult' families could be trained to behave in a more acceptable manner serves to underline the strong preference for tenants who 'fitted' council houses both physically and socially. The early ideal—that better houses made better people—had often been sustained by ensuring that most tenants were of a sort that would not challenge the ideal. Major Astor's 'fallen sister' had no place in allocation schemes which excluded unmarried mothers.

Councils varied considerably both in the criteria used to decide whether somebody was eligible at all for a council tenancy and in the degree to which they 'graded' their tenants as suitable for different quality houses. Those with large quantities of the same kind of houses at the same sort of rents need exercise less discretion than councils who needed to fill a range of less desirable properties, suitable only for less 'desirable' people. Their application records would be marked with 'suitable only for older property'; or 'housekeeping standard: fair/poor'. People who supposedly had priority through slum clearance or overcrowding might be excluded altogether by rules which, for example, discounted furnished tenants as 'transients'—and a 'dirty' family from a slum property would never be given a 'clean' house. [29]

---

28 Elizabeth Burney, *Housing on Trial* (London, OUP/Institute of Race Relations, 1969).

29 L Corinna looked at the social impact of selective allocation policies combined with large-scale demolition in *Housing Allocation Policy and its Effects: A Case Study from Oldham CDP* (York, University of York, Department of Social Administration and Social Work, 1976). One quote from a housing file sums up the approach. 'This is a good house. Do not let it to a scrubber'. See also Fred Gray's study of housing allocation in Hull, 'Selection and Allocation in Council Housing', *Transactions of the British Institute of Geographers*, 1976, New Series 1, 34-45.

But the council housing market took on a momentum of its own. As research in Sheffield[30] and elsewhere has shown, estates of similar age, style and quality acquired quite different degrees of 'desirability' in the eyes of would-be tenants. A variety of factors may be involved, but evidence suggests that 'reputations' of estates were—and are—easily made or marred by the perceived social habits of the residents. The arrival of an intake of former slum-dwellers, or even of one or two criminal families, might be enough to label certain estates, or individual streets or blocks within them, as places that would never willingly be chosen by people entering the council sector or transferring within it. The 'spiral of decline' referred to in a previous chapter might then set in. The scenario is a familiar one which will be considered further in a later part of this chapter. Amongst other things it lends economic credibility to the efforts of council landlords to prevent contamination of estates by 'undesirable tenants', if the result was likely to upset an organized social harmony and lead to loss of revenue from empty dwellings.

But council policies were sometimes directly responsible for the creation of such difficulties. For one thing, not all of them heeded advice against housing 'difficult tenants' all together in one place. Indeed, as hard-to-let pockets of public sector property emerged, this sometimes proved a convenient way of filling them. Housing officers and housing applicants came to share pretty much the same view of where different addresses stood on the social scale and the 'best' streets or blocks were effectively reserved for people worthy of them. Hence the social cachet of places such as the 'Brass Button' estate in Sheffield, so nick-named because tenants were drawn from the uniformed classes—bus drivers, policemen, postmen, park-keepers and other stalwarts of the social order.

An example of the opposite process occured in Luke Street, Crossley, near Liverpool, described by Owen Gill.[31] Although popular at first, this estate was the only one with houses big enough for very large families. As a result, it became the council's routine placement for families that were not only poor and numerous but (usually in consequence of these things) also facing social problems. They included several families on whom the police kept a particularly close eye. Taken all together, these factors quickly sent the reputation of Luke Street plummeting. In 1971 a

---

30 John Baldwin, 'Problem Housing Estates—Perceptions of Tenants, City Officials and Criminologists', *Social and Economic Administration*, vol.8, 1974, 116-135; A E Bottoms and P Wiles, 'Housing Tenure and Residential Crime Careers in Britain', in A Reiss and M Tonry, eds. op.cit.; A E Bottoms, Rob Mawby and Polii Xanthos, op. cit.

31 Owen Gill, *Luke Street: Housing Policy, Conflict and the Creation of a Delinquent Area* (London, Macmillan, 1977).

leaked council report said that parts of the estate had been used to 'rehouse the town's problem families, social misfits etc.' (Gill, p.24). This was confirmed by Gill's research in the housing department records, where housing visitors' notes on families being rehoused contained many comments such as 'Very poor type of family. Luke Street or similar' (p.26).

A standard work on housing management reissued as late as 1982 endorsed the practice of matching tenants to property on the basis of a visit to assess 'suitability'.[32] Well into the 1970s housing authorities were sifting and shifting tenants according to 'desert', although urged by the Cullingworth committee[33] in 1969 to make housing need their sole criterion and to abolish residential restrictions and 'grading' of tenants by housekeeping standards. The report recommended throwing council tenancies open to anyone and allocating them simply on date order, giving tenants a choice of properties at varying rents. The committee said it was:

> . . . surprised to find a number of housing authorities who took up a moralistic attitude towards applicants; the underlying philosophy seemed to be that council tenancies were to be given only to those who "deserved them". Thus unmarried mothers, cohabitees, "dirty" families and transients tended to be grouped together as "undesirable".

They believed that the practice of using housing visitors to make assessments 'leaves too much scope for personal prejudice and unconscious bias to be acceptable'. (Cullingworth recognised the issue of 'a minority of applicants with severe social problems' but had little to say about them except that their needs should be assessed by social services departments). But the liberalising agenda spelt out in the report was not heeded by council landlords until forced upon them by market conditions.

Private landlords take the strain

The exclusiveness of much council housing practice depended upon one thing: the continued existence of a large, varied, and above all cheap, private rented sector. Well into the second half of the century, the much reviled private landlord effectively preserved the status of council housing as the provider of homes for predominantly lower middle class and 'respectable' working class tenants. Rent control depressed

---

32 John Macey and Charles Baker, *Housing Management*, 4th ed. (London, *Estates Gazette*, 1982).

33 Central Housing Advisory Committee, *Council Housing Purposes, Priorities and Procedures, Ninth Report of the Housing Management Sub-Committee of the Central Housing Advisory Committee* (London, HMSO, 1969).

standards as well as prices but kept large tracts of old housing within the means of the poor. A 1962 survey, for example,[34] found that the median rent (net of rates and other charges) for council tenants was £65 per year compared with £44 for private unfurnished tenancies—even decontrolled rents were only £56. Furnished tenancies were not controlled, and in areas of shortage in the 1950s and 1960s the most accessible housing was usually an insecure furnished tenancy in a crudely sub-divided property. Large houses which had failed to attract affluent occupants had long been prone to slide down the social scale into working class tenements—as happened for example to spec-built Victorian terraces in parts of Notting Hill. People who might not be acceptable as conventional council tenants did not usually become homeless as long as there were sufficient low-standard private rentals for them to move into. Streets which provided cheap lodgings for large poor families could acquire bad reputations but still provide vital support networks for breadliners, and in this they were no different from many a 'sink' housing estate.[35]

The bottom end of the private sector offered little physical amenity but at least provided flexibility and, for those who sought it, anonymity. There was little defence against predatory or hostile neighbours and landlords. But neither were tenants subject to surveillance by social workers and housing managers. If they owed rent, the solution could be a moonlight flit. Most of the dwellings were not classifiable as slums, but some of the old prejudice against slum dwellers became transferred to people living in multi-occupied houses, even where housing shortages and council-house rules specifying local residence qualifications meant that these were the only homes available to newcomers.[36] The squeeze on owners of multi-occupied property by health and safety enforcement enhanced the attraction of selling to an owner occupier and thus contributed to the increase in homelessness in the 1970s.

---

34 J B Cullingworth op. cit., 45.
35 A brilliant social history of such an area is Jerry White's *The Worst Street in North London: Campbell Bunk, Islington, Between the Wars* (London, Routledge and Kegan Paul, 1986).
36 The Manchester Medical Officer of Health, Dr Metcalfe Browne, reporting in 1961, said that 'bad housing conditions are not infrequently associated with unemployment, poverty, a low standard of personal cleanliness and hygiene, defective maternal care, and ignorance and fecklessness. Such conditions are especially likely to flourish among an immigrant population, irrespective of colour or creed, with defective standards of hygeine and social conduct'. Cit. Burney, op. cit, 167.

Housing market change the key to social change

Profound changes in the structure of the housing market lay behind the eventual transformation of councils and other social landlords into providers of residual housing for socially disadvantaged groups. The prime factor was the rapid popularity of home ownership, encouraged by tax breaks. For many years after World War II, demand was substantially met by the selling off of older rented property to owner occupiers. This was the main reason for the decline in availability of private tenancies and the increased pressure within the sector, documented in 1965 by the Milner Holland report into housing in Greater London.[37]

Some former tenants could afford to buy but the rest could only turn to council landlords and the insignificant number of housing associations. Meanwhile owner-occupation was becoming more attractive to middle-income households who still formed a substantial proportion of council tenants. In 1961 the housing tenure of foremen and skilled manual employees was split fairly evenly into owner-occupation (37 per cent), local authority tenancy (32 per cent) and other tenancies (31 per cent). By 1981 the proportions were: 56 per cent; 35 per cent; and a mere nine per cent in shrunken private renting (including housing associations).[38]

During the process of transition,[39] there was actually more of a social mix throughout tenures than had existed before. But from the 1960s changes in policy and in the economy hastened the process of residualisation of social housing which has been its salient feature in the last years of the century. Income data illustrate the trend. In 1963 the proportion of households in the bottom three income deciles who were council tenants was 26 per cent; by 1979 it was 47 per cent.[40] In the following decade, as the size of the council stock shrank, the focus on poverty within it increased (*Table 1*). By the same token, ever increasing proportions of council tenants claimed income support. The unemployed and economically inactive had become enormously concentrated in the council sector, and in certain geographical areas within it. By 1993 nearly two-thirds of council tenants were in 'non-earner' households.[41]

---

37 Report of the Committee on Housing in Greater London, Cmd 2605 (London, HMSO, 1965).

38 Alan Holmans, *Housing Policy in Britain* (Aldershot, Croom Helm, 1987), 202.

39 Peter Lee and Alan Murie, *Poverty, Housing Tenure and Social Exclusion* (Bristol, University of Bristol Policy Press, 1997).

40 Peter Malpass and Alan Murie, *Housing Policy and Practice* (London, Macmillan, 4th edition 1994), 148.

41 Lee and Murie op. cit, 11.

Table 1: Income deciles of council tenants		
	1980	1991
percentage in:		
bottom decile	17	30
second decile	15	20
top three deciles	15	4

Source: Malpass and Murie, p.150.

Changing priorities

The huge amount of post-war council house building had meant that the slum dwellers and overcrowded families which local authorities were obliged to house could be accomodated in unpopular flats and estates if they were deemed unsuitable for, or unable to afford, anything better, while 'good' tenants were encouraged to transfer to new property. Thus were processes of internal social polarisation reinforced. People in the unfavoured estates, aware of the despised status of their homes, had less and less incentive to prevent vandalism, litter etc., and the downward 'spiral of decay' became more visible.[42]

A new era arrived with the Housing (Homeless Persons) Act 1977. This for the first time gave statutory priority in council housing to homeless people in certain categories, such as pregnant women, the elderly and families with children. Exclusiveness was officially at an end, and councils had to start taking on as tenants some of the sort of people whom previously they would have tried to avoid. Soon afterwards the new Conservative government, in the Housing Act 1980, introduced the 'right to buy' for council tenants—who could thus satisfy their desire to become owner-occupiers without moving house.

The combination of these two measures, and related legislation, did much to hasten the polarisation in the housing market which was already under way. The most 'desirable' council estates fairly soon became largely owner-occupied; more 'undesirable' tenants entered the remaining stock. Although it would clearly be a gross distortion to equate housing need with undesirable social habits, the point is that local councils now had less power to filter out potentially disruptive households. Some writers[43] have gone so far as to imply that the

---

42 E J Reade, op. cit.

43 See David Page, *Building for Communities. A Study of New Housing Association Estates* (York, Joseph Rowntree Foundation, 1993), 36. Page, however, is talking specifically about new estates, which by definition had no existing

obligation to give houses to people who needed them most has caused the crisis in social housing. This analysis ignores the magnetic pull of owner occupation which, starting long before the Housing (Homeless Persons) Act, reached an ever-widening social circle. Lee and Murie point out that the social profile of people on council waiting lists in recent years has been very similar to that of the homeless, and that economically they are alike distinguished by their inability to afford owner-occupation.

The pull of owner-occupation made it still harder to let dwellings on unpopular estates and blocks. Many post-war flatted estates had proved unpopular from the very start because of their design.[44] Unlettability became a much wider blight by the 1990s in the most economically distressed areas, on account of sheer depopulation. In northern England and south Wales huge tracts of otherwise reasonably attractive housing became empty and blighted; many were demolished, but it took a long time before the extent of the problem was acknowledged.

Local authority landlords had every reason to fill otherwise unlettable property with people, such as young single men, whom they would never before have considered as tenants. Everywhere, homeless people and other disadvantaged groups, such as single mothers, and ethnic minorities, were steered into areas which would be shunned by applicants with less urgent need. (The obligation to house the homeless did not mean they were treated equally; it was, and is, usual practice to give them only one 'take it or leave it' tenancy offer).

For a combination of reasons, therefore, there is no doubt that social housing managers have had to become used to working with a far more needy mix of tenants, of whom an increasing proportion, especially in the south-east of England, have been homeless. From the point of view of the present analysis, the question is how far the changing nature of access to council housing, by leaving managers with a reduced gate-keeping role, led eventually to the introduction of alternative methods of securing tenants' behaviour.

Not only did local authorities lose some of their control over whom to accept as tenants; even more importantly, they lost the ability to rid themselves of troublesome tenants more or less at will. Prior to the Housing Act of 1980, which introduced the *Tenants' Charter*, most local authority tenants had little or no security of tenure. From 1980, they acquired the same rights as protected tenants in the private sector. In order to evict a tenant a court order now had to be obtained, based on written grounds which had to conform to the list of acceptable grounds

tenants, who if present might have been less disadvantaged than new tenants nominated by local authorities.

44 Alice Coleman, *Utopia on Trial* (London, Hilary Shipman, 1985).

stated in the statute. Nuisance behaviour and using the premises for criminal purposes were among the possible grounds, but the procedure was cumbersome and expensive.

The 1980s saw more policy changes designed to create greater choice and autonomy for tenants—such as the right to choose to transfer their estates to alternative forms of ownership. The most immediate impact however was from the introduction in 1982 of means-tested housing benefit as the only form of rent subsidy. No longer need local authority landlords put poorest tenants in the cheapest houses, since with housing benefit footing the bill they could afford the best. One of the main rationales for differential allocation systems vanished and simultaneously a crippling poverty trap was created. Council rents shot up, further encouraging the better-off tenants who were not eligible for subsidy to move into owner-occupation, and discouraging unemployed people from seeking low paid work if it meant losing their rent subsidy. Thus was polarisation nudged further.

Given the changed role of the public sector in recent years, compounding the process of residualisation that had begun much earlier, it is perhaps surprising not that 'problem' estates have persisted—and become the focus of enormous expense and effort to turn them round—but that there are not more of them. As we have seen, the slide into 'problem' status was a process which evolved from practices which were endemic within the sector long before the big decline in popularity of council renting. By 1974, the government was already sufficiently concerned to carry out a survey of the number and nature of unpopular estates.[45] But this was against a background of the still stable nature of most of the rest of the public stock. Now, councils—and, increasingly, other social landlords—are having to cope with their most difficult estates on top of dealing with a much more vulnerable average set of tenants. The 1998 initiatives from the government's Social Exclusion Unit (which cites research identifying 1,370 council estates with concentrations of deprived households[46]) are only the latest in a series of policies which over 20 years have not solved the problem of marginal neighbourhoods.

By the late-1990s the flight from unpopular areas of social housing had in some areas of the country become a flood. Turnover of tenants and shifting around within the sector, as people sought more congenial environments, created increasing instability. Private renting was even coming back into favour as an alternative.[47] In the 20 years up to 1996,

---

45 *Difficult to Let* (Department of the Environment (unpublished), 1974).

46 *Mapping Local Authority Estates Using the 1991 Index of Local Conditions* (London, Department of the Environment 1997).

47 *Guardian,* 7 October 1998.

net turnover of council housing stock doubled.[48] As an increasing number of dwellings (within a shrinking total) remained empty, the term 'abandonment' entered the vocabulary of housing management. There were even examples of new, suburban-style social housing developments proving unlettable in parts of northern England.[49] Some blamed high rents, especially those charged by housing associations, which meant that private renting was once again becoming a competitive option for some families who would previously have had no choice other than social housing. But an important study of low demand in Manchester and Newcastle found pockets of abandoned housing across all tenures.[50] Reluctantly it was beginning to be recognised that programmes of demolition of council housing stock might have to be carried much further—even where, as in Glasgow, a huge debt burden remained on dwellings already demolished.

In this context the old relationship between social landlords and their tenants has been turned on its head. For most of its history, a council tenancy was something for which the tenant was deemed to be grateful, having passed some kind of test of worthiness. Now, the problem for many social housing landlords, outside areas of acute housing shortage, is to show that their property is an acceptable option for the 'respectable' working class. Other countries in Western Europe face like problems.[51] Commenting on the situation in Denmark, Lotte Jensen describes how market weakness has forced social landlords to 'woo' consumers.[52] The further that areas slide into marginality, exacerbated by unemployment, the harder this becomes.

The growth of new 'deals' which allow tenants more say in the running of estates is one consequence. Another is the promise of greater security, delivered in ways which include the control, or removal, of disruptive or criminal persons. The 'difficult tenant' has been rebranded as 'anti-social'; the 'problem family' has become the 'nuisance neighbour'.

---

48 Hal Pawson, 'Supply But No Demand'. *Inside Housing* 2 October 1998, 18-19. 'Net' turnover is defined as the number of relets to new tenants divided by the total housing stock. London is now the only area where turnover has levelled off. The north of England is the worst (mobility in Blackburn is described by Pawson as 'colossal').

49 *Guardian*, 10 November 1998.

50 Anne Power and Katherine Mumford, *The Slow Death of Great Cities?: Urban Abandonment and Urban Renaissance* (Joseph Rowntree Foundation, 1999).

51 Anne Power, 1997, op. cit.

52 Lotte Jensen, 'Cultural Theory and Democratising Functional Domains: The Case of Danish Housing', *Public Administration* Vol. 76 No.1 (1998), 117-139. Jensen argues that shifting the 'governance' of social housing onto the tenants will only work if they are sufficiently socialised to form a strong 'group' model.

Amongst other things the contractual relationship has been exploited for its potential in preventing not disease, as of old, but criminal behaviour (*Chapter 5*). In so doing, social landlords may have offered more than they can deliver. The extent of the difficulties involved are what we shall turn to next.

CHAPTER 3

Making Trouble

> Over the last generation, this has become a more divided country. While most areas have benefited from rising living standards, the poorest neighbourhoods have tended to become more rundown, more prone to crime, and more cut off from the labour market. The national picture conceals pockets of intense deprivation where the problems of unemployment and crime are acute and hopelessly tangled up with poor health, housing and education.
>
> (Social Exclusion Unit, *Bringing Britain Together: A National Strategy for Neighbourhood Renewal*, Cm 4045, September 1998).

The outcomes of growing geographical inequality in Britain have taken some time to be recognised for what they are, longer still to be approached in a holistic manner. The report from the government's Social Exclusion Unit takes known facts about deprived neighbourhoods and tries to show how they should be dealt with by means of a vast collective effort involving every responsible public agency working together at neighbourhood level with the people themselves. Policies which recognise multiple causes and joint responsibilities were long overdue, but the proposed course of action is still tentative and experimental. Meanwhile the symptoms of social deprivation, including those which suggest depletion of social order, will not disappear.

The quotation above brackets crime and unemployment twice in successive sentences; the linkage, though not necessarily straightforward, is no longer denied.[1] In particular the area profiles obtained from the British Crime Survey confirm the geographical confluence of indices of deprivation and concentrations of crime.[2] The containment of crime and disorder however cannot wait on economic rescue: the fire-fighting has to go on. This means that narrowly-focussed, short-term solutions to problems of lawlessness and social friction will continue to be used in places where the underlying structural deficiencies are too great to be overcome for many years to come. There

---

1 High youth unemployment is correlated with high crime levels: see John Wells, *Crime and Unemployment* (London, Employment Policy Institute, 1995); John Graham and Benjamin Bowling, *Young People and Crime*, Home Office Research Study 145 (London, HMSO, 1995). Local concentrations of unemployment resulting from deindustrialisation are also seen as weakening social ties. See summary in Tim Hope, 1996, op.cit.

2 Tim Hope, ibid.

is always a danger that over-dependence on these solutions will in turn be a source of distortion to social relations, and this is a question to which we will return later.

Meanwhile this chapter will look more closely at the nature of crime and disorder in deprived neighbourhoods, as it affects both residents and managers of social housing. Later chapters will describe a particular range of responses from central government and local authorities, which adopt a rule-making mode of reimposing order. Other responses cover a whole spectrum from 'heavy-end' policing—of hot spots and high profile suspects for instance—through physical target hardening, to social initiatives such as credit unions and training schemes. The following account emphasises both the vulnerability presented by the social and economic imbalance in certain neighbourhoods, and the types of predatory or nuisance behaviour to which this exposure gives rise. In adopting this focus one must not, however, lose sight of the point made in *Chapter 1* that people living in places with apparently similar high levels of crime may actually vary greatly in their feelings of insecurity.

In so far as it is possible to generalise about such places, it can be said that the neighbourhoods in which deprivation and insecurity tend to converge will contain various combinations of the following population features far in excess of national averages, and that all these imbalances will have increased in recent years:

- children living in households below the poverty line;

- unemployed, unqualified, young adults;

- single parent households;

- single adults, especially those formerly in institututional care;

- ethnic minorities, especially refugees;

- elderly poor.

The area will typically be one of instability and change, featuring:

- high turnover of households;

- rapid decline of local labour market in recent past;

- progressive loss of services such as shops and transport;

- visible deterioration of upkeep of buildings and public spaces; and/or

- patches of radical physical change: demolition/remodelling of housing stock.

The crime profile will typically be that of youthful perpetrators: vandalism, car crime and burglary. Some areas will experience a cluster of problems associated with illicit drugs. Occasionally more serious violence and intimidation will dominate small areas, centred on 'gangs' or certain families. Domestic violence and other forms of repeated victimisation are likely to be common.[3] Friction between neighbours may arise from the incompatibility of some of the population groups listed above. Nuisance-type complaints will predominantly be concerned with noise, litter, uncontrolled dogs and children, and rowdy youths. Very large concentrations of unemployed youths have the potential for semi-permanent disorder, which when it escalates into 'riot' is almost always triggered by some form of confrontation with police.[4]

Council rented tenure is well established as a correlate of criminality[5] and the youthfulness of the population is a large part of this. But tenure distinctions are blurred at the margins; statistically, the poorer owner occupiers are closer to council tenants on indices of deprivation and experience of crime than they are to owner occupiers in general.[6] Market decline and sharp increases in crime and disorder are particularly noticeable in some areas of old private housing, for instance in the north-west of England where there has always been more working-class owner-occupation. More directly relevant to the subject of this study is the growth of 'mixed tenure' within council-built estates; either through the operation of the 'right to buy', or through a deliberate policy of transferring or rebuilding sections of estates to provide for housing associations or private developments intended for owner occupiers. The use of varied ownership to help regenerate unpopular estates is but one of the many initiatives introduced to that end, all of which can be shown to have mixed success.

Estate improvement programmes, notably the centrally sponsored Priority Estates Programme (PEP) and its successor the Estates Action Programme, have striven to reverse the decline of unpopular estates

---

3 Hazel Genn, (1988), op. cit.; Kate Painter, 'Different Worlds: The Spatial, Temporal and Social Dimensions of Female Victimisation', in Evans, Fyfe and Herbert, eds., op.cit.

4 Anne Power and Rebecca Tunstall, *Dangerous Disorder: Riots and Violent Disturbances in 13 Areas of Britain, 1991-92* (York, Joseph Rowntree Foundation, 1997).

5 Anthony Bottoms and Paul Wiles, (1986), op. cit.

6 Alan Murie, 'The Housing Divide', *British Social Attitudes Survey* (Aldershot, Social and Community Planning Research, 1998).

throughout the 1980s and most of the 1990s. Most of the money and effort has gone into physical improvements and repairs, more responsive management, and, increasingly, tenants' views being taken into account. Visually many estates have been transformed (e.g. grey concrete flats magicked into pitch-roofed terrace houses with front gardens) and litter and graffiti much reduced. Improved physical security has been part of the package and there have been a large number of separate crime-prevention programmes and intiatives on estates.

Evaluations[7] show that, up to a point, all these things can make estates physically much more attractive and less intimidating, cleaner and with less environmental disorder. It is possible to reduce crime significantly, make tenants happier and even improve demand. But all of these gains are liable to be undermined by outside forces which increase social polarisation and leave tenants and managers struggling with higher levels of socially disruptive behaviour. It is noteworthy that almost all the neighbourhoods which were analysed following severe outbreaks of youthful disorder in 1991-2 had been recipients of extensive improvement programmes.[8]

The best account of the complex factors and influences within estates that were subject to the attentions of PEP comes in the Home Office research by Janet Foster and Tim Hope[9] in Hull and Tower Hamlets. They found that the benefits flowing from the programme in terms of crime reduction and community reinforcement were highly dependent not only on the background socio-economic situation but also on local characteristics which might vary even from one part of an estate to another. They concluded that:

> . . . there were two obstacles to the wider effectiveness of the PEP model on the estates studied: first, the 'quality' of implementation; and second, the instability of residential communities arising from population turnover, social heterogeneity and the "subterranean culture" within estate communities. (p.84)

7 For example: Anne Power and Rebecca Tunstall, *Swimming Against the Tide: Polarisation or Progress on 20 Unpopular Council Estates, 1980-1995* (York, Joseph Rowntree Foundation, 1995); Steve Osborn and Henry Shaftoe, *Safer Neighbourhoods?: Successes and Failures in Crime Prevention* (London, Safe Neighbourhoods Unit, 1995).

8 Anne Power and Rebecca Tunstall, (1995) op. cit.

9 Janet Foster and Tim Hope, *Housing, Community and Crime: The Impact of the Priority Estates Programme*, Home Office Research Study 131 (London, HMSO, 1993).

Population instability has long been noted as a negative influence on order and trust in any residential population[10]. The Hull case illustrates the destabilising effect of the 'double trouble' from unpopular properties (which have to be filled to meet financial targets) and the need to fill them with people in direst need, who are likely to be the most vulnerable and isolated individuals. In the study it became clear that a hated tower block had been used to house a number of young homeless men who became sucked into the local drug scene with knock-on effects for other residents.

Population instability and heterogeneity often render concepts of 'community' applied to estates fairly meaningless. Tenants' spokespeople may in reality speak for only a segment. Age, gender and ethnicity all tend towards different concepts of things like 'threat', 'safety' and 'nuisance'.[11] Newcomers are mistrusted and, as Walklate's study in Salford emphasises, living in a high crime area crucially depends upon knowing whom you can trust.[12]

Foster and Hope go on to observe:

> The reality of life on high crime estates is that "community" is socially fragmented . . . [The] more established and stable families . . . tended to keep themselves apart from the other, more vulnerable residents, especially the troubled and troublesome minorities. Indeed, their concern was to have these groups removed from their estate. In the light of this study, it would seem unrealistic to expect many residents to to be able or willing to exert much direct influence over the behaviour of those involved in crime and disorder on the estate. Thus the means to tackle the causes of that criminality which is directed by some residents against others may need to be sought elsewhere.

We know that the Hull scenario repeats itself in many impoverished areas and we may need to look no further for explanations of the rise in complaints of 'anti-social behaviour' and the pressure for exclusionary solutions. It is hardly surprising that housing managers have turned to one thing which they understand: tenancy rules and enforcement. Targeting individuals is within their remit, and especially if those individuals are behaving in such a way that unpopular housing becomes still less marketable (creating ever-bigger holes in the revenue account), it will be seen to serve a dual purpose.

---

10 John Baldwin and Anthony Bottoms, *The Urban Criminal* (London, Tavistock, 1976).

11 See Sally Merry, op.cit.

12 Sandra Walklate, 'Crime and Community: Fear or Trust?', *British Journal of Sociology*, vol. 49:4, December 1998, 550-569.

To say this in no way diminishes recognition of the task facing these managers, or the reality behind many of the complaints brought to them by tenants.[13] Some suffer from intolerable situations and many more from persistent incivilities. We will now look more closely at some of the specifics.

THE MAIN ELEMENTS OF ESTATE CRIME AND DISORDER

Much has been made of the appparent increase in 'neighbour nuisance' (*Chapter 4*). This has many component parts and some of them (at the more aggressive or damaging end of the spectrum) merge into actions which are clearly criminal. Nevertheless a distinction must be maintained between that which is criminal and that which does not merit that label, although recent legislation and the surrounding rhetoric (*Chapter 4*) appear deliberately to blur the distinction. Police attitudes may also have something to do with it. There has been an historic tendency on the part of the police to view neighbour and domestic 'incidents' as unworthy of serious attention. The lack of regular policing was, until comparatively recently, a particular feature of council estates, because patrolling was restricted to public highways, and the internal streets within estates were not part of the beat. Even in the 1980s policing on many 'problem' estates was only in response to emergencies.[14] Today these neighbourhoods may, in contrast, be subject to a variety of policing strategies—but often, still, with officers only intervening when forced to do so.

Because complaints about neighbours are more often mediated through neighbourhood housing offices than via the police or other agencies, they tend to be seen all together as 'management problems' rather than as discrete matters requiring a range of solutions. Hence the great variety of behaviour which for administrative convenience tends to be labelled 'anti-social' in the eyes of local government. A survey conducted by the Social Landlords Crime and Nuisance Group analysed 15,635 cases of 'anti-social behaviour' dealt with by 20 social landlords in

---

13 A housing manager on one estate, which had incidentally benefitted greatly from the Estates Action programme, remarked to the author that she could always tell the latest location for 'youth trouble' or drug nuisance 'because all the people in the waiting room will be from the same spot'.

14 Anne Power, 'Housing, Community and Crime' in D Downes, ed., op.cit.

1996/7.[15] The most common types were: noise, 33 per cent; garden disputes, 15 per cent; and criminal behaviour, nine per cent. Exactly what was included in this relatively small criminal element is not clear, since domestic violence, physical intimidation, drug abuse and harassment were all counted separately and together amounted to nearly 16 per cent of cases: which suggests that the 'civil' and 'criminal' distinction was not regarded as particularly important. What is evident, however, is that the traditional sources of friction between neighbours: noise, and gardens (where they exist) remain very high on the list.

Noise complaints can quite often be found to emanate from causes endemic in poor neighbourhoods. Here are some factually-based examples of noisy behaviour which households might complain about, each of which suggests a totally different series of possible remedies:

- Motor bikes roaring up and down late at night.
  Cause: unemployed youths.

- Groups of noisy and sometimes aggressive strangers frequenting the stairs.
  Cause: the drug dealer who lives opposite you.

- Shouting and violent behaviour heard though the party wall and sometimes spilling into the street.
  Cause: domestic strife/alcoholism.

- Footsteps pacing the room above and loud music playing in the small hours.
  Cause: the schizophrenic who lives above you has stopped his treatment and is plagued by 'voices' in his head. (There is also poor insulation between the floors).

- A dog that barks and howls all day in the next-door flat.
  Cause: your neighbours' fear of burglary, which has occurred on three occasions while they have been out at work.

Likewise, the variety of causes and meanings which underly actions grouped indiscriminately as 'mindless vandalism' is easily forgotten. Wilson and Kelling's[16] 'broken windows' theory implies something akin to a disease and ignores the range of human agencies involved. Much of

15 Social Landlords' Crime and Nuisance Group, *Anti-Social Behaviour in England, 1996/97: A Report on Patterns and Problems in Tackling Anti-social Neighbours* (Coventry, SLCNG, 1998).

16 James Q Wilson and George Kelling, op. cit.

the destruction on estates is far from mindless. The boy who broke your kitchen window with his football may have intended the backdoor as his goal. Or, your broken window may be the work of a frustrated burglar. There are many places where it could be the work of bullies—targeting you perhaps as somebody who is racially or somehow otherwise different or defenceless. Or it carries a message of retaliation from your neighbour whose child you reproved for damaging your fence. More sinisterly, it could be a warning from the local hard men that if you report their illegal activities you can expect something much worse than a window to be broken.[17]

Destruction of property is a side-effect of the illegal market in the most hard-to-manage estates. Empty properties are boarded up with notices stencilled on the shutters announcing that everything of value has been removed. Things are essentially no different from 100 years ago when the 'destructive classes' used stair rails for firewood and sold every bit of internal scrap metal that they could remove. Newly renovated houses are especially vulnerable and only huge cost and vigilance can prevent whole kitchens, bathrooms, electrical fittings and heating systems being removed for profit almost as soon as they are installed.Two councils are reported as having lost £575,000 between them in one year on looted boilers alone.[18] Another employs a security firm belonging to the erstwhile local crime boss, because it knows that if it buys its protection on that estate from another firm, its contractors will be targeted.[19]

Apparently pointless destruction does also occur. As one housing manager remarked to the author: 'I can understand them wanting the pipes but why do they have to completely destroy whole walls as well?'. Even derelict property has to be made safe against intruders who might cause fires and even endanger their own lives. No wonder some neighbourhood housing officers will say that 'vandalism' is the type of disorder which brings them the greatest management problem, although tenants might not have quite the same order of priority.

Among the many surveys of tenants' experiences in problematic housing areas, was one conducted in Brixton in 1996 by the National Council for the Care and Resettlement of Offenders (NACRO).[20] This

---

17 A similar typology is proposed in Stanley Cohen's 'Sociological Approaches to Vandalism' in *Vandalism: Behaviour and Motivations,* Claude Levy-Leboyer, ed. (Amsterdam, Elsevier Science Publishers, 1984).

18 *Inside Housing,* 4 September 1998.

19 Personal communication.

20 Mark Liddle, Frank Warburton and Mark Feloy, *Nuisance Problems in Brixton: Describing Local Experiences, Designing Effective Solutions* (London, NACRO,

focussed expressly on nuisance and anti-social behaviour in four council-owned estates. One of the marked impressions gained from this study is that, although most people when asked about specific types of unpleasantness will have experienced a wide range, individually their main focus of complaint varies quite a lot, along with the particular characteristics and immediate environment of their household, as well as their own age, race and gender. Yet at the same time there was a linkage between many of the common complaints. As the researchers state: 'The context in which nuisance problems arise is probably a crucial prerequisite to effective intervention. . . . the research also suggests that nuisance problems are usually both highly localised, . . . and interconnected'

Litter, graffiti, noise (mainly loud music), and abandoned/badly parked cars were common themes which, however, were experienced most intensely by only by a few. Even the 'nuisance' impact of illicit drug selling and usage was at its worst in only a few well-defined areas, especially one block where people came to inject, leaving blood and needles behind. Only 18 out of 282 households interviewed put drugs at the top of the list of 'what is bad' about the estate. (A similar survey in Merseyside or Central Scotland would certainly yield more intense concern about drug use, which still impacts very differently in different parts of the country).

In other words, local versions of generalised problems have to be dealt with appropriately; and 'effective responses are likely to require a flexible, multi-faceted approach' says the report, which also contains the results of a survey of local authority responses to nuisance behaviour. The report's detailed recommendations will be considered further in another chapter. It is clear thus far that legal remedies alone cannot be a sufficient or effective response to anti-social and nuisance behaviour which stem so pre-eminently from wider social phenomena.

'YOUTH TROUBLE'

The Brixton tenants frequently expressed various concerns about the behaviour of young people, but were not necessarily cowed into silence. As many as 47 per cent said that they had intervened 'to stop kids or teenagers misbehaving' in the past 12 months. Despite reports of intimidation from young people, some of the incidents where adults claimed to have intervened were quite serious, including attacks and muggings. For many households however 'youth trouble' was their main

1997). Some of the points quoted are from the fuller, unpublished, version of this report.

local worry. A black African woman bringing up three children on her own identified 'teenagers misbehaving and bullying' as the issues of most concern to her, whereas an older white woman on another estate said that the worst thing she had to put up with was children playing football outside her flat, 'but you daren't get angry with them for fear of reprisals'. Of these two women, therefore, the anxieties of the first were for her children while the second was troubled by children. In both cases it was the intimidating behaviour of groups of young people causing the problems. A focus group of young people, when asked about their own problems, felt that the local tenants' association was a nuisance in denying them occasional access to the facilities of the tenants' hall, given that there was 'nothing for us' on the estate. However, far and away their greatest 'nuisance' was in the form of frequent stops and rough treatment by the police (remember this was Brixton, where mutual suspicion between police and young black people has been embedded for more than a generation). The report identifies the various anxieties about youth as a connecting theme in several types of crime and nuisance complained of, and puts this in the context of more generalised feelings of insecurity and lack of personal ties on the estates expressed in the survey.

'Children misbehaving' or 'youths hanging about' are recurrent complaints in tenant surveys in all parts of the country, echoing standard themes of the disorder paradigm. W J Wilson attributes the lack of informal social control of children in poor crime-ridden neighbourhoods to the withdrawal of institutional support to families.[21] As Pitts and Hope remark,[22] this places extra burdens of responsibility on families with reduced capability. Poverty makes supervision harder for parents[23] and lack of supervision has strong links with delinquency.[24] Unsupervised groups of young children roaming on an estate can through sheer mischief cause disproportionately serious effects, for instance through setting fires (though removing rubbish can reduce this particular problem). More importantly they are subject to many hazards to their own health and safety. Quotes from the most deprived areas visited by members of the Social Exclusion team include the following example:

---

21 W J Wilson, *When Work Disappears: The World of the New Urban Poor* (New York, Knopf, 1996).

22 op.cit p 41.

23 Harriet Wilson 'Parental Supervision: A Neglected Aspect of Delinquency', *British Journal of Criminology*, vol. 20, 1980, 203-235.

24 Loraine Gelsthorpe summarises the literature on this issue in 'Parents and Criminal Children' in *What is a Parent?: A Socio-Legal Analysis*, A Bainham, S Day Sclater and M Richards, eds. (Oxford, Hart Publishing, 1999).

Gangs of kids harassing you on the streets outside shops. Seven and eight year olds, sleeping out all night with cans of lager is common. They light a fire under the bridge and sniff gas. There is loads of glue sniffing round here. It's getting to the stage that more are doing it than not. The police just haven't got time for people like us.[25]

The sense of young children 'out of control' has produced a punitive legal response in the Crime and Disorder Act 1998, which allows for area child curfews, child safety orders and parenting orders, and for anti-social behaviour orders on children as young as ten.

Groups of older youths may be seen in a more menacing light. The failure of the job market deprives young men of adult roles and, as Graham and Bowling found[26], delinquent habits of teenage years are no longer outgrown by the early twenties. A process of what has been described as 'criminal embeddedness' becomes established in lieu of any transition into employment.[27] Violence ensues when, as Hope and Pitts observe, conflicts established at school are continued in later years: younger teenagers get sucked in and 'the school becomes a forum for the enactment of neighbourhood conflict'.[28]

Disorderly groups of young men and boys may be identified as a menace even in peaceful middle-class areas[29], but on some impoverished estates they appear to fill a power vacuum. For Beatrix Campbell[30], in her study of some of the communities which spawned the disorders of 1991-1992 , the question is: who is in charge? Assertive groups of young males pose a conscious challenge which, if no effective behavioural boundaries exist, can swell into the prevailing power in a neighbourhood—the 'Goliath' of Campbell's title. She writes: 'The crisis of the estates is spatialised when the young men assert their dominance by flooding the public domain, primarily the streets, with their own, exclusive, coteries . . . Control over space is used to dominate' (p.318). Dominate whom? perhaps we should ask, remembering the differing reactions observed by Walklate in different parts of Salford to the presence of young men: here an estate which actually featured in one of the worst 'riots' was one where people felt no threat from their own 'boys'.

---

25 op. cit., 32.
26 John Graham and Benjamin Bowling, op. cit.
27 Tim Hope 1996 op. cit., 184.
28 op. cit. 1997, 39.
29 Ian Loader *et al*, op. cit. 1998.
30 op.cit. (1993).

SUBSTANCE ABUSE AND DRUG DEALING.

In areas like north-west England or Central Scotland, drug strategies are central to dealing with manifestations of neighbourhood nuisance in a sense which is less pressing in, say, inner London (though local patterns of hard drug use are currently changing fast[31]). Although drug misuse can be found among all regions and levels of affluence, and many different substances are involved, the association of heroin, in particular, with areas of deprivation and high unemployment has been evident for years.[32] The 1996 *British Crime Survey* found twice as many young drug users among the unemployed.[33] Pearson's 1980s research in north-western England mapped small pockets of extreme poverty and social need which, in most cases, corresponded to the neighbourhoods where heroin was most embedded. There was a clear connection with multi-problem housing areas with bad reputations where hard-to-let dwellings were filled by drug misusers and other marginal groups.

Drug markets easily become established where there is an existing criminal economy, sucking in local youth.[34] From many examples it can be seen how the drug market can go on to overwhelm a neighbourhood. Serious dealing can involve violence, intimidation and no-go public spaces. Small-scale user-dealing is far commoner, but if conducted from the home may bring invasion of semi-private space, noise and crowds at late hours, and repulsive detritus, especially where injecting is involved. Police action seldom has more than a short term effect, or may simply serve to disperse and even exacerbate rather than reduce the problem.[35] In the early heroin 'epidemics' communities turned, in vain, to the health

---

31 Howard Parker, Catherine Bury and Roy Egginton, *New Heroin Outbreaks Among Young People in England and Wales*, Police Research Group, Crime Prevention and Detection Series, Paper 92 (London, Home Office, 1998).

32 H Parker, K Bakx and R Newcombe, *Living With Heroin: The Impact of a Drugs "Epidemic" on an English Community* (Milton Keynes, Open University, 1988); Geoffrey Pearson, 'Social Deprivation, Unemployment, and Patterns of Heroin Use' in *A Land Fit for Heroin? Drug Policies, Prevention and Practice*, N Dorn and N South, eds. (Basingstoke, Macmillan, 1987).

33 Malcolm Ramsay and Josephine Spiller, *Drug Misuse Declared in 1996: Latest Results from the British Crime Survey*, Home Office Research Study 172 (London, Home Office, 1997).

34 Angela Burr, 'An Inner-city Community Response to Heroin Use', in S McGregor, ed., *Drugs and British Society* (London, Routledge, 1989).

35 N Dorn, K Murji and N South, *Traffickers: Drug Markets and Law Enforcement* (London, Routledge, 1992); L Sherman and D Rogan 'Deterrent Effects of Police Raids on Crack Houses: A Randomized, Controlled Experiment', *Justice Quarterly*, vol. 12, 1995, 755-781.

services to 'cure' the problem;[36] now, they are more likely to complain to their local housing manager. Landlords cannot ignore drug-induced nuisance, but need to work with other agencies in dealing with individual abusers.

The extremes to which professional drug dealers on estates can go to make themselves impregnable is illustrated in the allegations made against the defendant in the case of *Bristol City Council v. Lovell.*[37] Mr Lovell was a tenant whose attempt to exercise the right to buy his house became entwined with the council's efforts to repossess on the grounds that he was using the premises as a base for selling drugs—said to have furnished the means for his desired purchase. The fact that the council had acknowledged his right to buy before giving notice of the intention to seek a possession order provided the basis for a long drawn out legal battle eventually decided by the House of Lords in favour of Bristol City Council. It was alleged that the house:

> . . . has been suitably adapted to the [drugs] trade, with steel grilles over doors and windows, kennels for Rottweiler dogs, surveillance cameras to check visitors, a radio scanner tuned in to police frequency and equipment for locating covert listening devices'. (HLR 98, 776).

A commonly-favoured option when councils are faced with concentrated drug dealing in specific streets or blocks of flats is simply to raze the site—a traditional response which has been used in the past to expunge 'red light' property.[38] Clearly this does nothing to prevent replication of the problem elsewhere. One reason why housing authorities in the most drug-prone areas have repeatedly resorted to 'crime control by bulldozer' is that they tend to be the areas already overburdened with unwanted housing.

INTIMIDATION, HARASSMENT AND RACISM

Close residential proximity of victims and perpetrators is self-evident in neighbour disputes and often extends to other types of aggravation and violence as well. Intimidation has been identified as a major obstacle to obtaining court witnesses in both civil and criminal cases in troubled areas; this has indeed become the *raison d'etre* of lowering the standard of proof required to establish 'anti-social behaviour' in section 1 Crime and Disorder Act 1998 (*Chapter 5*). In practice it is quite hard to distinguish the extent of 'intimidation' as compared with the traditional 'no grassing'

---

36 Angela Burr, op. cit.
37 House of Lords, 30 HLR 1998.
38 See the example quoted by Anne Power (1987), op. cit., 51.

culture of many communities accustomed to unfriendly policing, as well as the natural reticence which people may have in pursuing actions against neighbours. But there is no doubt at all that many potential witnesses are deliberately put in fear and that threats and violence are in some areas the routine experience of victims who dare to report a crime, while those who are prepared to use 'heavy' methods remain immune from prosecution. The extent of the problem is hard to gauge. A house-to-house survey on five high crime estates carried out by the Home Office found that in 13 per cent of crimes reported by the victims and nine per cent by other witnesses intimidation followed, while 28 per cent of potential witnesses (including six per cent of victims) did not report for fear of intimidation.[39] There are bound to be problems with this kind of research: people may be too afraid to speak even to a researcher; and conversely, some victimisation may be assumed to be a form of intimidation when it is not.

Determined and concerted action has been taken by police and local councils to protect witnesses in some of the worst cases, where a few individuals were responsible for terrorising an estate[40] though a far commoner response is simply to rehouse the victim. Breaking through a strong anti-police culture has also been achieved, it is claimed, through intensive community policing of one estate with a traditionally 'bad' image (Meadowell, Tyneside)[41]. At a more general level, Salford Witness Support Scheme, featured in the report *Speaking Up For Justice*[42] aims to raise awareness across all relevant agencies of the need to overcome the

---

39 W Maynard, *Witness Intimidation: Strategies for Prevention*, Police Research Group Crime Detection and Prevention Series Paper 55 (London, Home Office 1994).

40 Sheridan Morris, *Policing Problem Housing Estates*, Police Research Group, Crime Detection and Prevention Series, Paper 74 (London, Home Office, 1996). See *Chapter 5* for more on this subject.

41 Ibid, 20-27.

42 *Speaking Up For Justice*, Report of the Interdepartmental Working Group on the Treatment of Vulnerable or Intimidated Witnesses in the Criminal Justice System (London, Home Office, 1998).

barriers which prevent witnesses coming foward[43] (in a city where intimidation has been extreme in some areas of private housing[44]).

Harassment and bullying, often directed at people who are vulnerable or in some way different, are probably the worst features of life in places where they are endemic. Though by no means confined to racial minority victims, these groups are certainly among the most exposed and a long history of racist persecution on council estates is more researched than it is resolved.[45] Racial incidents recorded by housing authorities give only a partial picture[46] and are often poorly handled. For example Tower Hamlets, a part of East London with a long history of overt racism, only evicted a tenant for racial harassment for the first time in 1998. An action research project to protect victims of repeated racial harrassment on one estate in that borough, in the early 1990s, had found that police visits to the homes of perpetrators and warnings by the housing department to tenants that they were in breach of their tenancy agreement, did seem to deter the majority of perpetrators (but not the worst ones). Most perpetrators were close neighbours to, and many attended the same school as, their victims.[47]

A case from Lancaster, which has belatedly become a national scandal, is that of an Asian shopkeeper and his partner, an English woman, who suffered years of persecution from local youth, without any effective action from the police or the local authority.[48] Finally, in 1996, a 'Mischief Night' crowd besieged and petrol bombed the premises. Forty

---

43 The chairman of the Salford scheme, Anne Weir, has stated: 'I was born and raised in Salford and during my school years was exposed to the "No grassing" culture, where young people followed a code of honour which stated that if you were caught committing a crime you did not "Grass" on your accomplices. This culture appears to have changed over the last few years and the term "Grass" is now used to describe anyone who reports a crime and this includes victims, to the authorities and creates a feeling of fear' (cited in *Speaking Up for Justice*, p.244).

44 Author's own research.

45 Benjamin Bowling, *Violent Racism* (Oxford, Clarendon Press, 1998).

46 A Love and K Kirby, *Racial Incidents in Council Housing: The Local Authority Response* (London, Department of the Environment, 1994). A study on an East London estate found that although more racial incidents were reported to the housing office than to the police, more still were reported to the local law centre: Alice Sampson and Coretta Phillips, *Multiple Victimisation: Racial Attacks on an East London Estate*, Police Research Group, Crime Prevention and Detection Series, Paper 36 (London, Home Office, 1992).

47 Alice Sampson and Coretta Phillips, *Reducing Repeat Victimisation on an East London Estate*, Police Research Group, Crime Detection and Prevention Series, Paper 67 (London, Home Office, 1995).

48 *Guardian*, 1 March 1999.

convictions including several custodial sentences followed, but Mr Hussein did not succeed in obtaining damages from the council for failure to take effective action against the ringleaders.[49]

People suffering from mental disorders, who frequently get rehoused on unpopular estates and then left without support, are a group with a high degree of vulnerability.[50] They may attract hostility just for being 'strange' or cause trouble themselves to neighbours and housing officers, either through unpredictable behaviour or sheer inability to cope with ordinary household routines like cleaning and rubbish disposal, resulting in nuisance complaints. In turn they suffer break-ins and vandalism (especially while away in hospital) and sometimes violence. In one survey, 36 per cent of tenants with mental health problems reported harrassment by neighbours and 32 per cent found neighbours 'difficult to get on with'.[51]

FAMILY BUSINESS

Reports of anti-social behaviour on estates are littered with references to families. The 'family from hell' is a folk-devil, featured in the local press and in voyeuristic television programmes. Truly horrible neighbours they may be, but it still makes uncomfortable viewing to see a woman and children being jeered by a gleeful crowd as they are evicted from their home.[52] In Scotland, the notorious Haney family move from place to place: in Bannockburn they were 'driven out within hours of moving in'.[53] These headline cases would probably have been 'problem families' or 'difficult tenants' in the 1930s, 1950s or 1970s too. People who attract these labels tend to be dysfunctional in many ways and their unpleasant behaviour just one manifestation.

Frances Reynold's research in 1981-1983 on a 'problem estate' where there was continual friction between 'rough' and 'respectable' families[54] found exactly the same kinds of behaviour being complained of as in more recent typologies of 'nuisance neighbours'. Only a few of her 'rough' families fell into her category of 'anti-social': 'people who were

49 *Hussain and Livingstone v Lancaster City Council*, 31 HLR (1999), 164-186. See also *Chapter 6*.

50 Elizabeth Burney and Geoffrey Pearson, 'Mentally Disordered Offenders: Finding the Focus for Diversion', *Howard Journal*, vol. 34 no. 4, November 1995, 291-313.

51 Revolving Doors Agency, *Risk Factors in Tenancy Breakdown for People with Mental Health Problems* (London, 1997).

52 BBC 1, *Panorama*, 'Nicking the Neighbours', 30 March 1998.

53 *Inside Housing*, 21 August 1998.

54 Frances Reynolds, *The Problem Housing Estate* (Aldershot, Gower, 1986).

indifferent or hostile to their neighbours, who did not seem to care how much their behaviour upset or inconvenienced others, and who would verbally or even physically attack those who complained'. (p.177). One such family, themselves inveterate complainers, 'felt hated and victimised and responded by directing hate and suspicion to everybody on the estate and all the agencies they were involved with' (p.62).

The nasty neighbour may or may not be part of a 'criminal family'— another frequently encountered but ill-defined category. It is beyond the scope of this book to explore the making of outlaw dynasties, as some of these appear to be. It is noticeable however that a description frequently applied (and this may be true in some parts of the country more than others) is that of 'tinker' or 'gypsy'—in other words the stereotypical 'outsider' defiantly entrenched in a non-conforming life-style. That this style may sometimes embrace adaptive modes well-suited to low-work economies is seldom appreciated, least of all by neighbours annoyed by activities such as recycling second-hand car parts in the front garden. The travelling lifestyle has been effectively criminalised in recent legislation, notably the Criminal Justice and Public Order Act 1994[55]. Settled former travellers are often no more welcome.

Families of the type likely to be labelled 'anti-social' can be extensive and very supportive of each other. It may be the shortage of these qualities in other sections of the community which makes it possible for them to take charge. Police and local authorities sometimes join forces to drive out families who are terrorising estates. Often the pressure on them causes them to leave of their own accord, sometimes into the private sector,[56] where they may still raise alarm.

Families with a criminal tradition who may cope very well in their own terms need to be distinguished from non-coping 'problem families'. The latter, often people whose housekeeping and rent-paying was a mess, used to be taken in hand by social services, but now may be only monitored over child protection concerns. The same kind of people may easily get into rows with neighbours, sometimes being unable to deal with social situations in a non-aggressive way. But strategies which enable 'nuisance neighbours', where possible, to develop less abrasive habits are surely preferable to mere expulsion.

The Dundee Families Project offers a prototype of how families whose behaviour is likely to lead to eviction can be coached into more

---

55 Sue Campbell, 'Gypsies: The Criminalisation of a Way of Life?', *Criminal Law Review*, 1995, 28-37.

56 One example was Jack Straw's 'Family X' from Blackburn (cited in *A Quiet Life: Tough Action on Criminal Neighbours*, Labour Party, 1995). There are a number of anecdotes about evicted families causing trouble and/or meeting with hostility in the private sector, but no proper research on the subject.

pro-social habits. This is a partnership between the local authority's housing and social services departments and a voluntary body, 'NCH Action for Children'. Families under threat of losing their tenancies through legal action are given help according to their needs—such as parenting skills, anger management and managing their tenancy. A small number are taken into a core unit or placed in special dispersed housing, but the majority remain in their existing homes. After the first two years of operation 41 families who had been under threat of eviction were now living securely in their homes with the threat removed and three families who had received intensive help in the core block had returned to mainstream housing.[57]

Family support services have for years been acknowledged as the key to resolving a range of social problems and are proclaimed as central to turn-of-century government policies. The government consultation paper *Supporting Families*[58] recognises the extra effort that has to be put into the most needy areas and proposes more intensive and co-ordinated support for very young children and their parents in a 'Sure Start' programme. The consultation paper proposes, among many other things, an enhanced role for health visitors extending beyond the first weeks of a baby's life and a range of 'good parenting' intiatives. If all this means more resources for poor neighbourhoods it is good news. Less good, perhaps, is the fact that the paper emanates not from the Department of Health but from the Home Office, whose recent policies for parents and children have been punitive rather than supportive. There is a fine line, as always, between helping and controlling.

---

57 Personal communication.
58 London, Stationery Office, 1998.

CHAPTER 4

'Something Must be Done'

In the mid 1990s political momentum gathered pace behind a generalised fear of crime and dislike of yobbish behaviour. The prospect of a coming election encouraged the Labour party to stake its claim to the ground where crime and yobbishness converged. Its policies were fuelled by some particularly bad local experiences in areas of high unemployment and destabilised communities. The Conservatives had already shown that there was a political appetite for legislation directed at nuisance behaviour, tapping in to a media-fed public perception that the most obnoxious versions were pervasive and increasing, but also supported by evidence of fast-growing numbers of complaints. This chapter will focus on the political response and the manner in which it has been translated into legislation providing new mechanisms for behaviour control, enshrining new objects of public obloquy. It is the backcloth to the specific response in the field of social housing which is described in detail in the next chapter.

Earlier chapters have described how relatively few housing areas have come to contain extremely high levels of crime and nuisance, with exceptional experience of repeat victimisation—especially inter-personal — being suffered by a minority of the inhabitants. It is the concentration more than the nature of the unpleasantness that makes these places different. Because there are similar features to be found in a much larger spread of neighbourhoods, and the concept of the 'neighbour from hell' can apply in any social setting, public concern is readily roused. The use of elastic terms such as 'neighbour nuisance' and 'anti-social behaviour' can be applied to almost anything we dislike or disapprove of. The anxieties of the majority find expression in appropriating these labels to their own set of suspicions and grievances. Many people are annoyed by such things as litter, parking on the pavement and loud music played by neighbours. The qualitative difference which exists in certain extreme local situations is seldomed conveyed when news stories spread them to a wider public, to whom they may represent a generalised threat, or confirmation of a perceived decline in social responsibility.

There are a number of ways of cutting this cake. 'Neighbour disputes', as Karn et al[1] point out, 'are inseparable from the wider issue of 'nuisance' which appears to be a matter of growing concern'. Crime can also be involved with either or both of these. The situation can be

---

1 V Karn, R Lickiss, D Hughes and J Crawley, *Neighbour Disputes: Responses by Social Landlords* (Coventry, Institute of Housing, 1993), 1.

presented diagramatically in the form of three overlapping circles labelled 'neighbours', 'nuisance' and 'crime'.

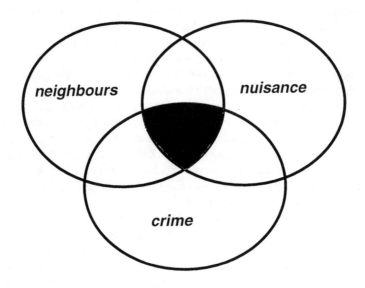

The worst area is that section where all three overlap—the nuisance is crime-related and emanates from your neighbours. Such is the situation of someone who lives on the same staircase as a drug dealer whose customers throng the landing and leave used syringes on the stairs; anyone who complains gets threatened verbally or with a brick through the window.

Crime and nuisance also overlap in ways which are not neighbour-related—much vandalism comes into this category. Equally, and most commonly, 'neighbours' may create (or be perceived as creating) 'nuisance' or annoyance which is outside the sphere of crime altogether. The rise of the term 'anti-social behaviour', discussed below, is essentially a blaming mechanism attached to a cluster of unwelcome phenomena which are loosely associated with each other.

How is it then that there seems now to be such a public reaction against a range of social irritants—it may be the behaviour of your neighbour's children or his dog or the way he quarrels loudly with his wife—which have existed whenever and wherever people have lived side by side? Are figures such as the 271,000 complaints against neighbour nuisance estimated to have been received by local authorities in 1995[2] only the tip of an iceberg? A book devoted to new ways of socio-legal regulation has to raise such questions even if it cannot answer them. An earlier chapter has touched on some of the features of present-day society in which traditional social ties seem weakened and people may therefore feel more defenceless, defensive and uneasy. There are also physical and technological aspects of modern life which contribute new hazards to tranquillity, and specific social structures which cause them to impinge harder on certain people.

There is another side to the coin, however. If people complain more it may be because they feel empowered to do so. They may be more vocal and demanding of the agencies responsible for delivering services because this is actively encouraged in the managerialist culture of government which sets standards, devises measures of accountability and treats citizens as consumers. More telephones, more help desks and more information help to turn grumblers into complainers.

Why noise?
It is highly significant that a large component of neighbourhood nuisance complaints concern noise. Control of domestic noise escalated during the 1980s from a primarily technical problem to a simmering political issue, driven by the rising number of complaints. There was no particular social or geographical identity attached to the issue; given the widely different contexts involved anybody could appropriate this concern as their own. Noise is a stereotypical middle-class issue and though it may well be that working class neighbourhoods suffer more from noise, the middle-class appeal ensures that the subject receives attention. When 'noise' connects with 'neighbours' as well as with 'nuisance' there is potential for a popular campaign.

Noise is therefore where it is most appropriate to begin when trying to analyse the constituent parts of 'anti-social behaviour' and the new methods of regulation to which it has given rise. It is also a field in which mediation clearly offers an alternative approach to resolving disputes (see below), with a considerable track record, although this essentially

---

2 James Dignan, Angela Sorsby and James Hibbert, *Neighbour Disputes: Comparing the Cost Effectiveness of Mediation and Alternative Approaches* (Sheffield, University of Sheffield, Centre for Criminological and Legal Research, 1996).

low-key response has not had the same political appeal as methods which apportion blame and punishment.

The figures collected every year by the Chartered Institute of Environmental Health suggest that complaints about domestic noise in England and Wales rose ninefold between 1978 and 1995/96—from nearly 18,000 to 164,000—and that they are still rising at around 10 per cent every year.[3] Scottish experience also shows noise at the top of the 'anti-social' league.[4]

Figures like these have raised political pressure, but they need to be treated with caution. Each year over 40 per cent of local authorities fail to respond to the CIEH questionnaire about noise complaints, and these include some of the larger urban councils. Those which do respond differ from year to year. There is no standard system for logging complaints, and no way of allowing for duplication—so if several people complain about one noise, or one person complains several times, each complaint is still counted as a new one. On the other hand, according to a Building Research Establishment (BRE) survey in 1991,[5] only 3.6 per cent of people who were bothered by neighbour noise actually made a complaint to the authorities. They were more likely to approach the neighbour directly—although a few said that they were too frightened even to do this.

Mediation services consistently deal with noise-related disputes more than anything else—42 per cent of their referrals according to the Sheffield University survey of the cost-effectiveness of mediation in neighbour disputes.[6] The same survey found that noise was the cause of 62 per cent of the complaints of neighbour nuisance made to Environmental Health Departments. Housing departments receive a different mix of complaints, but noise still predominates: a survey of social landlords by Salford University, cited by Karn *et al*[7] found that 25 per cent of tenants' complaints against neighbours were about household noise and a further seven per cent 'children's noise'. In Scotland, Clapham *et al* found that domestic noise and noisy parties headed the list of neighbour disputes in social housing—the latter probably reflecting

---

3 Chartered Institute of Environmental Health, annual series.
4 Scottish Affairs Committee, *Housing and Anti-Social Behaviour* (Parliamentary Papers, HC 160, 1996); David Clapham, Keith Kintrea, John Malcolm, Hilary Parkey and Suzie Scott, *A Baseline Study of Housing Management in Scotland*, Centre for Housing Research and Urban Studies, University of Glasgow (Edinburgh, Scottish Office Central Research Unit, 1995).
5 Building Research Establishment, *Effects of Environmental Noise on People at Home: BRE Information Paper 22/93* (Construction Research Communications Ltd., 1993).
6 Dignan *et al*, op. cit.
7 Karn *et al*, op. cit., 2-4.

the high proportion of flatted accomodation in Scotland. However, when the focus shifts away from neighbours on to dislikes about the wider area, noise comes only seventh, according to a York University 1998 survey, with crime, dogs, and leisure facilities, in that order, ranking highest.[8]

Is there anything about today's noisy neighbours which makes them different from those who have been the subject of complaint since urbanisation began? Broken down into its components, modern neighbour noise has a very large element of amplified music, which together with barking dogs heads the list of causes of friction.[9] Many surveys have confirmed these two things as the major aural irritants from neighbours especially in high density flatted accomodation (see for example NACRO's Brixton survey cited in *Chapter 3*). More people may leave dogs alone to guard their homes for fear of burglary. Sound systems are many times more powerful than they used to be and more widely available.

Stereos, televisions, washing machines and DIY equipment are all relative newcomers to the home and capable of carrying though poorly insulated walls and floors. A good deal can be done to improve insulation, and case law has shown that landlords can be liable for nuisance generated by poor sound-proofing.[10] It is less easy to govern cultural and lifestyle differences in which clashes of behaviour are sometimes exacerbated by prejudice—against the young or against ethnic minorities for example. Increased employment in unsocial hours means that domestic activities may be carried out all round the clock. Unemployed people may also tend to nocturnal habits. A writer in *The Big Issue* recently described life on Lincoln Green estate in Leeds:

> We have two distinct sections of the community: one that lives during the day and sleeps at night, generally the employed and elderly; and those that live during the night and sleep during the day. These are usually the alcoholics, drug users/pushers, and the young unemployed. Those who have to work during the day are disturbed by fights, cars coming and going and people playing loud music. Police raids and car chases are also a regular occurrence.[11]

People normally regard it as their right not to be prevented from sleep, and may be less tolerant than they used to be about other degrees of disturbance. Different sorts of noise arouse different strength of feeling: neighbour noise is much more annoying than aircraft or traffic for

---

8 Burrows and Rhodes, op.cit.
9 Dignan *et al*, 1996, op. cit.
10 E.g. *Baxter v Camden London Borough Council* (1998), 30 HLR 501.
11 Kathy Tebbutt, 'Estate of the Nation', *The Big Issue,* June 22-28 1998, 24.

instance (BRE, 1991)—and is sometimes, rightly or wrongly, perceived as harassment. Environmental health officers, surveyed by the National Society for Clean Air and Environmental Protection (NSCA) in 1998,[12] were largely of the opinion that rising expectations (85 per cent) and incompatible lifestyles (76 per cent) were the main reasons for the increase in noise complaints. They believed that the public had unrealistic expectations about noise levels (80 per cent). Only about half the respondents thought that inadequate sound insulation and more powerful sound equipment had much to do with the rise in complaints. If this assessment is correct, it suggests that we should be more careful than ever about prescribing policies on the basis of statistics of complaints by neighbours.

In reality it may be impossible to disentangle the degree of disturbance created by noise with the disapproval or dislike projected on to its source, since they are largely interdependent. The strong bass beat of much popular music, enhanced by amplification, is enjoyed by some people as a liberating form of self-expression at the same time as for others it is a potent source of conflict and cultural challenge.[13] As with any perceived nuisance, intensity grows with frequency of repetition. For many reasons, intrusive music has come to epitomise the concept of anti-social behaviour and, as political pressure against noise nuisance mounted, amplified music became a focus for new forms of legal intervention .

The search for solutions

Noise control in general, and domestic noise in particular, is subject to fairly frequent government review, and whatever systems are in force the inexorable rise in complaints appears to create the need for new methods. The Noise Review Working Party of 1990 ('the Batho Committee')[14] is reckoned to have aired the subject thoroughly. It noted that complaints to local authorities about noise from domestic sources had increased fivefold in the decade to 1988, in spite of the duty laid on local authorities in sections 57 and 58 Control of Pollution Act 1974 to serve an abatement notice where they were satisfied that nuisance from noise existed or was likely to occur.

The committee considered a number of ways to reduce the problem: better insulation; publicity and education; encouraging people in neighbourhoods to work together on noise; new legislation; and effective

---

12 *NSCA Noise Survey 1998* (Brighton, National Society for Clean Air and Environmental Protection, 1998).
13 Loud music was associated with drugs in the decision to criminalise 'raves' in the Criminal Justice and Public Order Act 1994.
14 *Report of the Noise Review Working Party 1990* (London, HMSO, 1990).

enforcement. One suggestion put forward to the working party by the UK Environmental Lawyers Association (UKELA) was for Neighbourhood Noise Watch schemes on the lines of the existing anti-crime Neighbourhood Watch, as a means of encouraging local solidarity and social responsibility with regard to noise. This was considered worthy of further investigation but the report warned:

> The analogy should not be pushed too far. Current neighbourhood watch schemes are based upon a rallying together against a common and external menace. A noise watch scheme on the other hand would be intended to set a standard of neighbourly behaviour within a community whose individual members might have rather different views of what was acceptable.

This observation touches on the core themes of 'neighbour nuisance'—differing standards of behaviour, and the unsettling presence of 'the enemy within', themes which recur throughout this study. For similar reasons, the working party rejected the idea that by majority agreement residents in an area could set and enforce their own noise limits.

Having rejected the more aggressive use of private law, the Batho committee also considered whether 'deliberate, sustained and excessive' noise should be made a criminal offence. Both they and UKELA took the view that the problems of definition were too great to introduce standards of criminal proof. The Home Office was not encouraging, knowing that the police, never over-anxious to intervene in quarrels between neighbours, did not want to be forced into controlling domestic noise. There was therefore a general consensus that noise should continue to be dealt with entirely in the context of the law of nuisance, where an offence only occurs once a notice of abatement has been flouted. The nearest that the Batho report got to the criminal law was to recommend 'consideration' of a direct offence, not requiring a prior abatement notice, 'where an owner or occupier knowingly or through negligence permits the use of his or her premises for a purpose giving rise to a noise nuisance'.

Enforcement powers were what needed strengthening, and also the will to use them. The Environmental Protection Act 1990 (passed while Batho was still deliberating) did go some way along this road. Local authorities now had a duty 'to take such steps as were reasonably practicable' (section 79(1)) to investigate complaints of statutory nuisance brought to them by residents of their area; it followed, as in the previous legislation, that they had a duty to act if following their investigations they were satisfied that a nuisance had occurred or was likely to occur. That meant serving an abatement notice—section 80 of the EPA strengthened the conditions in which this could be done and speeded up magistrates' court proceedings if the notice was flouted.

Failure to comply with an abatement notice was a criminal offence under section 80(4) with a maximum fine at level 5 (section 80(5)).

But the resources devoted by local authorities to investigation and enforcement were limited and very unevenly applied. Not for nothing had the words 'reasonably practical' been inserted into section 79(1) EPA 1990; local authorities had jibbed at the resource implications of an unqualified duty to investigate complaints of statutory nuisance. Some environmental health departments did receive complaints out of hours and operated patrols at weekends and on summer evenings armed with noise measuring equipment. But mostly, as Batho discovered, enforcement was only obtainable during office hours, when it was least likely to be needed.

The local authority response was much influenced by financial and political priorities. Manchester was one of the first authorities to try a multi-agency approach (police, housing and environmental health) to control the use of loud sound systems on estates. In Lambeth, although noise was also high on the political agenda, there was little co-ordination. Budget cuts in the early 1990s (and the rival claims of EU food regulations) meant the loss of weekend noise patrols. There were other complications: the most vociferous tenants' groups were sometimes seen as being racially motivated, and the council's race relations advisors urged caution in applying curbs which would be likely to lead to yet more black youths being prosecuted. This encouraged a 'step-by-step' approach to loud music and noisy parties in the borough; informal warnings were allowed time to work before any formal notice was served. The environmental health officers who operated the system found that in most cases a reasoned approach was enough to evoke a reasonable response—the few 'hard cases' were the problem.[15] In any case there were many inner city areas where neither the EHOs or the police wanted to run the perceived risks to personal safety and public order involved in hard enforcement, especially not direct intervention at the height of a party. Unspoken racial tensions were also involved.[16] Their view may have informed the Batho committee when it said:

> To attempt to take enforcement action while such a party is in full swing may lead to public disorder and may be dangerous for enforcement officers. . . . The problem is exacerbated by the tendency of people organizing such parties to remain in the background.

---

15 Personal communication.

16 The author's own voluntary work in Lambeth in the 1980s and early 1990s brought knowledge of the racial tensions associated with sound systems.

In Scotland a more robust attitude obtained. The Civic Government (Scotland) Act 1982 allowed a uniformed constable to take action relating to noise created by music, TV, or operating equipment. When noise from these sources gives 'any other person reasonable cause for annoyance' (no particular noise level is specified) the police officer can issue a warning and if the person responsible does not immediately desist an offence is committed. The Crime and Disorder Act 1998 strengthened the powers of Scottish police to enter premises and if necessary confiscate equipment.

Like much else at this time, partly through press and television coverage, noise became a rallying point for the well-behaved majority against the ill-mannered few. In the hot summer of 1995 *The Mail on Sunday* ran a campaign which helped to raise the profile of the issue, with headlines such as 'Thugs bring terror to the war on noise' and 'Father dies in all night music row'. It reported violence against enforcement officers in Ealing, St Leonards, Wolverhampton and Sandwell. In Harlesden, 40 policemen came to back up two enforcement officers called to an all-night party. A Manchester man died of a heart attack after a family row with a drum-playing neighbour. A pressure group based in Erith, the Right to Peace and Quiet Campaign, said 'The Government must act quickly to prevent the loss of further lives.' Fifty thousand readers wrote in to support *The Mail on Sunday's* call for £40 spot fines on noise-makers, as the heatwave caused complaints to proliferate.[17]

Meanwhile the Department of Environment, five years after the Environmental Protection Act 1990, had been reviewing the effectiveness of control of noisy neighbours.[18] It concluded that local authorities needed good practice guidance and should publicise their services better. There was a need to raise public awareness about acceptable noise levels. More night-time services were required and better liaison with police. The most important recommendation was that confiscation powers, both temporary and permanent, should be available to local authorities. Finally, the question of criminalisation was revisited and the report recommended consideration of a separate criminal offence for night-time noise nuisance.

It was therefore very much with Government blessing that in February 1996 Mr Harry Greenway, Conservative Member for Ealing North, introduced his Bill, which became the Noise Act, making excessive noise from domestic premises at night a criminal offence. He

17 *The Mail on Sunday,* 2 July, 13 August and 21 August 1995.
18 Neighbour Noise Working Party, *Review of the Effectiveness of Neighbour Noise Controls: Conclusions and Recommendations* (Department of Environment, Welsh Office and Scottish Office, March 1995).

paid tribute to the campaign in *The Mail on Sunday* and to the Right to Peace and Quiet Campaign. Between them these sources had publicised a number of horror stories, such as

> . . . that of Mrs Edwards. She would roam in a park near her home to escape the sound of a stereo blasting from the flat above her until 5 a.m. every night. After sitting out in the cold and rain for several nights, she died from a combination of pneumonia and despair.[19]

There had even been a number of murders attributed to disputes over noise, including one at a party firebombed by a neighbour.[20] The MP for Halesowen and Stourbridge, Warren Hawksley, echoing a statistic from *The Mail on Sunday*, stated that 'there have been 20 deaths as the result of agitation caused by noise since 1992'. Tony Banks, MP for Newham, knew of 'numerous examples' where noise had been used deliberately as a form of harrassment designed to drive somebody out of their home (this of course is a not uncommon allegation in landlord and tenant disputes). Clearly noise was by now well established as a favoured weapon of society's enemies, who must therefore be disarmed.

The Noise Act, which received royal assent in July 1996, is a measure which local authorities choose whether or not to adopt—on the grounds that local needs vary greatly (so what is a crime in one city may not be in the adjoining suburb). Authorities which adopt the Act take on the obligation to take reasonable steps to investigate complaints of excessive noise from a dwelling between the hours of 11 p.m. and 7 a.m.—in other words, they are in effect obliged to run a 24-hour noise control service. Armed with specialist equipment as specified in the Act, the environmental health officer must attend the site of the noise and measure whether it exceeds a set standard. The Act for the first time set precise decibel and time-span measures based on the World Health Organization guideline for proper sleep. Warning notices are issued on the spot and, if the noise is repeated before 7 a.m., it becomes a criminal offence with a fine up to £1,000 (level 3), but alternatively a fixed penalty notice, set initially at £40, can be served. Clause 10 allows for the seizure and (if a court so orders) the forfeiture of offending equipment. It also extends the power of seizure to noise nuisance being dealt with under the EPA 1990.

A strong body of opinion among the enforcers themselves, the environmental health officers, took the view that the Noise Act was not necessary, especially now that seizure of equipment was available to back up EPA action. There was criticism of the sound level as arbitrary

---

19 *Hansard,* 16 February 1996, col. 1248.
20 *Guardian,* 28 September 1995.

and of the law only being enforceable through on-the-spot measurement, as compared with the hearsay evidence permissable under nuisance powers. Even the minority of local councils who had expressed the intention to implement the Act have often not done so. By 1998 only eight local authorities out of the 241 responding to the NSCA questionnaire (a 57 per cent response rate) had implemented the Act. These were predominantly London boroughs, where it must be assumed the problem of night noise was greatest.[21]

Other noise controls, operated under nuisance powers, may have improved under the stimulus of the Noise Act—the NSCA 1998 survey found a wide range of different services, including at night, but few dedicated staff. Seizure of sound equipment was a much more popular option, and half of responding authorities said they had done this under the revised EPA. In view of the concern about attacks on enforcement staff, the 1997 survey also asked about the incidence of violence. Only five per cent of authorities reported that staff had been subject to assault, although abuse and threats were much more common. But 26 per cent said that fears for staff safety was a factor inhibiting night-time services (a year later this had gone down to ten per cent).

All the publicity concerning noise awareness and local authority powers seems to have encouraged a large response in terms of the level of complaints, even though as a publicised issue noise seems to have run out of steam. Many of these may be the product of frustration, since the resources devoted to noise control have not matched the heightened profile of the issue. This means that the question of further criminalisation may prove politically popular, although without large resources there is absolutely no likelihood of reducing noise by this means. Most local authorities still believe that the nuisance law is the most appropriate instrument, and that the problem will only be reduced through education.[22] (NSCA, 1998).

The recent history of noise nuisance has been described at some length because it provides a paradigm of the 'something must be done' issue. A source of everyday irritation, exacerbated by changing living and leisure patterns, acquires official status first of all through the availability of official channels of complaint, and subsequently through media reports and campaigns, providing a platform for political posturing and the justification for legislation which is presented as the essential 'crackdown' weapon. It turns out to be of little use except in a few localities, but meanwhile the enforcing professionals have been encouraged to use established methods more zealously. People grumble

---

21 NSCA op.cit.
22 Ibid.

on, but the political head of steam is exhausted. Politicians have to look for 'something else to be done'.

Will this paradigm fit the eventual history of the anti-social behaviour order? There are differences, as we shall see, especially concerning the availability of objective measures and attitudes within local government. Time will tell.

LEGISLATING AGAINST HARRASSMENT

It is useful briefly to examine another new law introduced into Parliament in 1996, again in response to public anxiety about particular behaviour patterns: the Protection from Harassment Act 1997. A few well-publicised cases highlighted the psychological harm inflicted by so-called 'stalking'—persistent shadowing of victims, usually with sexual undertones. This measure has been criticised for its manipulation of the concept of assault and for its unusual combination of civil and criminal law. In effect, the harassment must have occurred on at least two occasions and there are two levels of criminal offence: a purely summary (and usually non-violent) one, carrying a maximum punishment of six months' imprisonment; and an 'either way' offence, carrying a maximum of five years, where violence or threats of violence are involved. No proof of intent to harass or frighten is necessarily required. The lower level of harassment, 'actual or apprehended', may also be restrained through a civil injunction obtained by the victim, but if this is breached an imprisonable offence (maximum five years) is committed (when this aspect is in force). It is a prime example of legislation conceived in the spirit of 'something must be done' without reference to existing legal principles and options. A penetrating critique by Celia Wells[23] concludes:

> On one view the offences created by the 1997 Act are significant additions to the already extensive calendar of criminal offences with clear implications for both stalking and other forms of harassment. On another, there is little here that is not already covered by public order offences or by the 1861 [Offences Against the Person] Act as now interpreted. There are important underlying issues at stake. Criminal laws and criminal enforcement are at the front line of any society's struggle to understand and cope with conflict within and beyond its bounds . . . [There] is a strange unity between those who call for legislation on the grounds that the law is inadequate and those who decry what they see as judicial licence in extending the law. Both subscribe to a view of criminal law which is difficult to match with its practice—a view which elevates minimal *mens rea* requirements to

---

23 Celia Wells, 'Stalking: The Criminal Law Response', *Criminal Law Review*, 463-470, 1997.

something more, which ignores the extensive use of public order offences to supplement assault and injury offences, and which assumes that the law solves social problems.

The important issues raised by Celia Wells—especially her caveat against the assumption that the law can be used to solve social problems—are much to be borne in mind as we explore the legislative climate surrounding the Crime and Disorder Act and its targetting of 'anti-social behaviour'. It is salutary to observe that the Protection from Harassment Act has been used against a number of people far removed from the 'stalker' image—hunt saboteurs for example.

More to the point in the light of this study, in May 1998 two 13 year-old boys were convicted in Leicester Youth Court under section 2 of the Protection From Harassment Act 1997. It was reported by *The Times*[24] that 'the two boys and another teenager had led a campaign of hate against a family whose lives had been plagued by gangs for almost seven years'. The harassment consisted of 'almost constant bullying and round the clock intimidation, including swearing and stone-throwing' over an eight-week period. The pair were sentenced to 12 hour attendance-centre orders and their parents bound over to exercise care and control. As the report noted, the case 'highlights how a law designed primarily to stop stalking can be used against nuisance neighbours and persistent racial abusers'.

The Protection from Harassment Act therefore provides yet another option, and in this case it seems an appropriate one, for dealing with the sort of persistent bullying where victims become the accepted target for local children almost as a neighbourhood sport. (For an even worse example of this kind see *Hussain v Lancaster DC*, above pp.67-68 and below p.130). But it would be a big step to predict that successful prosecutions can do much to promote the attitudinal shifts necessary to eradicate bullying and racial harassment.

WHAT IS ANTI-SOCIAL BEHAVIOUR?

Before examining the genesis of the anti-social behaviour order, now enshrined in section 1 Crime and Disorder Act 1998, it is relevant to try to deconstruct the vocabulary involved. The epithet 'anti-social' could readily be applied to the behaviour of the two Leicester boys described above. But when, in the CDA 1998, a loose conceptual term is appropriated as a legal category there is considerable scope for confusion. This is especially so because the concept of 'anti-social

---

24 *The Times*, 22 May 1998.

behaviour' has travelled a long way in the past few years. Like a snowball rolling downhill, it has collected from its path an assortment of disparate items, which, becoming part of the growing mass, assume a common identity. Yet the nature of that identity remains imprecise, with different definitions of what is meant by 'anti-social behaviour' running concurrently in the public discourse. Paradoxically the reference in CDA 1998 section 1, to acting 'in a manner that caused, or was likely to cause, harassment, alarm, or distress', which borrows language from the Public Order Act 1986[25] (in turn much criticised when introduced), is looser than some of the meanings imputed in other fora where the problem is being addressed. The housing charity Shelter, for example, defines anti-social behaviour as occurring as 'the direct result of behaviour by one household or individuals in an area which threatens the physical or mental health, safety or security of other households or individuals'. Yet even this description could be used in the context of almost any kind of interpersonal conflict.

The difficulty with trying to pin down exact meanings for a widely used pejorative term is that 'anti-social' is a word which carries different weight according to its context. It first appeared at the beginning of the nineteenth century, associated with condemnation of revolutionary ideas.[26] In the past century totalitarian regimes have used it against their opponents—the Nazis put 'anti-socials' into concentration camps. It also carries a somewhat different meaning as a description of retreatist attitudes. By the end of the Victorian era it had become a sociological and psychological description of deviance but was also then being used to describe minor rule-breaking. Conduct that merely offends polite mores may be described as 'anti-social'. As a convenient label for irritating or disruptive activity, or sometimes more seriously regarded actions, the phrase 'anti-social behaviour' has been a familiar one for a good many years. It is a concept which transposes easily from disapproval of the action to disapproval of the actor, and vice versa.

---

25 Section 5 POA 1986. One result was that the charge of threatening or disorderly conduct 'within the hearing or sight of a person likely to be caused harassment, alarm or distress' was used by the police when they themselves were the only people present as potential victims. Tim Newburn, David Brown and Debbie Crisp, 'Policing the Streets', *HORS Bulletin* 29, 10-17 (London, Home Office, 1990).

26 The earliest reference in the Oxford English Dictionary (2nd ed. 1989) is from 1802: 'rebellious, anti-social, blasphemous . . . books'. Later references include a Fabian Society essay (1889), 'some kinds of anti-social action are so unreasonable . . . that we brand them as insane' and the Westminster Gazette (1904): 'to insist on not paying when asked by the conductor is at once inconvenient and anti-social'.

It is no surprise that the use of the term in the context of neighbourhood nuisance has been mediated by social landlords. The need to deal with conduct causing annoyance to other tenants is an integral part of their job and always has been.[27] The arrival of official usage of the phrase 'anti-social behaviour' seems to have co-incided with modern concerns about the fragilility of social control on housing estates. For example a Department of Environment advisory report in 1980, *Security on Council Estates*,[28] encouraged housing managers to walk their own streets, and in so doing 'anti-social behaviour can be noted and, where necessary, parents or the police can be informed of wrong-doers'.

This advice presents a picture in which a housing manager's duties included a bit of finger wagging at fairly low-key misbehaviour and where parents and police could be relied upon to take appropriate action. Ten or 15 years later, on the kind of estates described in an earlier chapter, the frequency and severity of the behaviour which might be designated 'anti-social' placed far greater demands on managers. Many of them would claim that neither parents or police would necessarily be of any help.

Qualitatively, change was for the worse under the influence not only of reduced informal social controls but also the arrival of two new elements—drug-dealers, and people suffering from mental disorders who had been discharged into 'community care' but left unsupported. At the same time, the decentralising of management into neighbourhood offices, and the new channels of dialogue being opened with tenants, forced them to receive and log ever more complaints from tenants against each other. As Karn *et al* [29] observe.

> [There] is pressure from tenants of local authorities and housing associations (or their neighbours) for landlords to enforce conventional standards of behaviour on their tenants. There is frequently an expectation from the public that to achieve this the landlord has ready recourse to legal powers and remedies. This expectation is not usually fulfilled and grievances against neighbours are often translated into grievances against the landlord if they do not or cannot find a solution.

Being blamed for not controlling bad behaviour and feeling unable to do so built up frustration within local government. Moreover when action

---

27 Among the more bizarre examples, Washington Urban District Council in 1927 handled complaints about one tenant who held loud spiritualist meetings and another who kept an unruly goat. Robert Ryder, op.cit.   ⟍

28 Housing Services Advisory Group, *Security on Council Estates* (London, Department of Environment, 1980).

29 Op. cit., 5.

was taken it was time-consuming and expensive.[30] Tenants began to complain to the Local Government Ombudsman about protracted failure to deal with nuisance neighbours, and some compensation awards were made. The ombudsman for the Midlands, Jerry White, reported: '[the] fundamental need, in almost every case, is for the council to co-ordinate effectively the various services involved and to devise and implement a plan for dealing with the nuisance'.[31] But councils often claimed that their hands were tied. Their demands for more freedom of action and swifter legal procedures in relation to tenants resulted in the Housing Act 1996 and other developments described in the next chapter.

The birth of the anti-social behaviour order

On introducing the Crime and Disorder Bill to the House of Commons on 8 April 1998 the Home Secretary, Jack Straw, famously declared that it represented 'a triumph of community politics over detached metropolitan élites'. In other words, the government knew about the pain of poor voters in crime-ridden neighbourhoods in a way that their critics, focussing on things like due process and human rights, were blind to. His statement accurately reflects the direct influence on government policy of the complaints voiced in constituency surgeries and, especially, the assertion by a strong group of Labour-led councils that what they needed was more powers, over and above the significant increase in controls which the Conservatives had given them in the Housing Act 1996.

Certain local authorities with some of the worst problems of estate disorder and crime had taken the lead in devising tougher remedies. In 1995 the Chartered Institute of Housing, the professional body whose members are primarily involved in the management of social rented housing, held its annual conference at Harrogate at which a fringe meeting focussed on the need for more determined action against people who were causing serious trouble in a variety of ways on certain estates. Ten member authorities, who were to become the core of the lobby for stronger powers in the new housing legislation, formed the Local Authority Working Group on Anti-social Behaviour (quickly to become known as 'ASB'). However they did not supply a definition of the term. Membership of the group grew (the name was changed to 'Social Landlords Crime and Nuisance Group' to reflect the inclusion of housing

---

30 Dignan *et al*, op. cit.
31 *Local Government Ombudsman Annual Report 1996/7* (London, The Commission for Local Administration in England, 1997), 17. The Chairman of the Commission, Mr Osmotherly, who handles cases from south-eastern England, also described at length his dealings with neighbour nuisance complaints, 9-10.

associations) and it became established as the most powerful lobby in the field, with (by 1998) a full-time administrator and assistant, based in the Coventry housing department, and publishing a newsletter, *Nuisance News*.

Peter Griffiths, Coventry's housing manager, had been a prime mover in establishing the lobby, and found a ready ear in the shadow Home Secretary, Jack Straw. Coventry had recently obtained *ex parte* injunctions against two of its more notorious tenants, the Finnie brothers—the case is detailed in a later chapter. This case was very influential in Labour party circles, where it chimed with some extreme examples of persistent local misbehaviour picked up from constituency surgeries. Although some Labour authorities, such as Hackney and Nottingham, had already shown that it was possible, in partnership with the police, to use existing powers to rid estates of serious crime and disorder,[32] the urge to present something different was irresistible. Once the policy opportunity was spotted, it was quickly developed. In June 1995 the Labour party, then in opposition, published its discussion paper *A Quiet Life: Tough Action on Criminal Neighbours.* This contained the outline of proposed legislation 'to restrain criminal anti-social behaviour by individuals or groups', on the grounds that existing criminal procedures were inadequate to deal with 'chronic and persistent anti-social criminal behaviour'. The Finnie case was quoted at length. It thus seemed quite clear that what was being talked about was criminal behaviour, and the proposals were drawn up on the premise that it was individual criminals who must be dealt with in order to restore the 'quiet life'.

The document outlined a proposed new order, which it called the 'community safety order', a form of civil injunction which could be brought by police or local authority and which carried criminal penalties of up to seven years imprisonment if breached. Conduct such as that of the Finnies was clearly criminal. But the document ranged broadly over non-criminal issues such as noise nuisance. One example described behaviour which at a slightly later date might have been labelled 'stalking' and which would have come within the scope of the Conservative government's subsequent anti-harassment legislation. The law eventually introduced when Labour came to power was closely modelled on the discussion paper but it refrained from defining anti-social behaviour in terms restricted to criminal activities, and was drawn up on much broader terms. The change of name from 'community safety order' to 'anti-social behaviour order' (ASBO) signifies a broadening of scope beyond that of crime prevention into matters more pertaining to nuisance control. Perhaps regretting this change of emphasis in the Act,

---

32 Sheridan Morris, op. cit.

the subsequent Home Office guidance on ASBOs reintroduced the gloss of criminality as the trigger for the order, talking of 'criminal or sub-criminal behaviour'[33]

The vivid illustrations of 'anti-social behaviour' used to heighten the argument in *A Quiet Life* were drawn from the casebooks of local authorities, mostly among those involved in the ASB Working Group, and all of them Labour controlled and able therefore to influence party thinking. As well as Coventry they included Jack Straw's constituency of Blackburn where the notorious 'Family X' provided much of the basis for the new policy. The discussion document described the terror inspired by this family, said to have clocked up two evictions and 54 arrests between them, for offences ranging from attempted robbery to public disorder, 'but their frequent court appearances rarely ended in much more than a fine, conditional discharge or other non-custodial sentence', said to reflect the weight of the individual offences rather than the conduct as a whole. (Interestingly the same examples, though unidentified, were recycled in 1999 to illustrate the Home Office guidance on ASBOs[34])

The Labour party document went on to say that its proposals had been drawn up after discussions with advisors to Coventry City Council and '[though] they were successful in [the Finnie] case, they are the first to argue that existing procedures are defective'. In the event, Coventry's success was short-lived. Early in 1996 the injunction against the Finnies was lifted, because the City could not raise the necessary witnesses to uphold it against appeal. Coventry's Director of Housing pressed the Labour party to pursue their plans for new legislation. It was said that the failure of the witnesses had been due to intimidation.[35] The Labour spokesman, Nick Raynsford, introduced a version of his party's proposed new order as an amendment to the Housing Bill, then at committee stage. This was substantially different from the eventual Labour government's version, in that it sought to make precise definitions. The prerequisites for imposing the order were to be: five 'unlawful acts' (crime or tort) within the area; five convictions for damaging social landlords' property; or five public order offences. It provided seven separate types of prohibition which might be contained in an order.

33　*Crime and Disorder Act: Guidance on Anti-Social Behaviour Orders* (London, Home Office, 1999). It is worth noting that the original draft of this guidance, sent out for consultation, was softer in tone, especially with regard to the use of ASBOs against the young.

34　op. cit, 'Case A' and 'Case B'.

35　HOC Standing Committee G, 29 February 1996, col. 432.

The amendment was rejected, as was another concerning witness protection, the Conservatives arguing that existing law was sufficient. The member for Normanton, William O'Brien asked:

> The Minister makes light of [the] proposals to try and protect our estates; what is his alternative? Is it to leave the estates as they are? Do the Government propose to do nothing about the problems suffered by people on estates because of a hard core of criminals?

Was Labour's policy really directed against 'a hard core of criminals' or something else? By the time Labour came to power and issued details of the proposed new order, in a a consultation paper of September 1997[36] it was clear that they had shifted ground from a criminal to a public order focus. The paper opened with the statement:

> Anti-social behaviour causes distress and misery to innocent, law-abiding people — and undermines the communities in which they live. Neighbourhood harassment by individuals or groups, often under the influence of alcohol or drugs, has often reached unacceptable levels, and revealed a serious gap in the ability of the authorities to tackle this social menace.

The paper went on to acknowledge that existing powers, under the Housing Act 1996 and the Protection from Harassment Act 1997 could be used in some circumstances (limited in the case of the Housing Act to the locality of social housing) but that these did not necessarily cover 'situations where the harassment is directed at a community rather than an individual or family, or where the behaviour is anti-social but not necessarily harassing'. Harassing 'the community' is a concept hard to distinguish from offences of public order against which the statute book is already well-provided. The lack of clear thinking behind the new policy was a likely cause of future trouble.

A different way in Scotland
There was a marked contrast to the approach adopted in Scotland. Policy-making in Scotland, prior to the existence of a Scottish Parliament, has been somewhat detached from day-to-day politics and largely controlled by the civil service. Debate in certain fields has been lengthy and serious, through committees, commissioned research, good practice manuals and discussion papers emanating from departments, universities or professional bodies rather than party headquarters. It so happens that neighbour disputes and anti-social behaviour in the housing context have been thoroughly examined in Scotland in recent

36 Home Office, *Community Safety Order: A Consultation Paper*, September 1997.

years resulting in a comprehensive body of published material examining the issues.[37]

In England and Wales, the only comparable detail is on the question of noise, which although an important part of the picture is only one element involved. There has been one other important study: into the cost-effectiveness of mediation in neighbour disputes carried out for Mediation UK by Sheffield University.[38] The latter produced the only available evidence for England and Wales of the extent of serious harassment and serious criminal activity involved in complaints about neighbours to council departments, estimated at five to five per cent of housing officers' caseloads. Much greater proportions of complaints to council departments involved life style or personality clashes, minor harassment connected with disputes, and sheer inconsiderate behaviour; all of which might be more suited to mediation than legal intervention. There was a notable lack of government interest in this kind of research prior to the drafting of the Crime and Disorder Bill.

The most significant Scottish examination of the issues involved was the inquiry by the Parliamentary Scottish Affairs Committee into Housing and Anti-Social Behaviour which took place from October 1995 to June 1996. The Labour Party had already published *A Quiet Life,* and one has the distinct impression that the Scots wanted to define their own priorities in advance of any future English-inspired legislation. The subsequent report and minutes of evidence supply a wealth of information and opinion on such questions as 'What is anti-social behaviour?'; 'Should it be distinguished from criminal behaviour?'; 'Is it increasing?'; 'What are the causes?'; 'How has it been dealt with by landlords?'; 'Should the law be changed?'. The contrast with the sketchy and anecdotal basis of the eventual government policy could not be greater.

Significant differences emerged over definitions. Glasgow City Council warned:

> The current debate on anti-social behaviour seems to be taking place in the context of confusion of ideas and problems so that it is not clear what the proposed solutions are expected to achieve . . . There are three distinct kinds of activity that are commonly discussed together as if they were the same thing:
> — Neighbour disputes.
> — Anti-social behaviour.
> — Criminal activities.
> These should be treated separately.

---

37 Clapham *et al,* op. cit ; Scottish Affairs Committee, op. cit.; Scottish Office 1998 op.cit.

38 Dignan *et al,* op. cit.

The memorandum from the Scottish branch of the Chartered Institute of Housing, however, argued somewhat differently:

> The Chartered Institute do not think it is particularly helpful to use one term (whether neighbour nuisance or anti-social behaviour) to cover a wide spectrum of behaviour ranging from action such as not keeping the garden tidy, to burglary, violence or drug dealing.
>
> We feel it more appropriate to define anti-social behaviour as actions which include behaviour which may often be criminal and should involve the police — such as drug dealing, unprovoked assault, racial harassment, vandalism and damage to property. We would prefer the term nuisance to be applied to less serious, albeit often annoying, behaviour such as lack of control over pets, stair cleaning, garden upkeep and verbal harassment.

Several witnesses to the Scottish inquiry linked anti-social behaviour to concentrations of deprivation, failures of community care, and drug abuse. The emotive and imprecise nature of the concept, and its dangers, were condemned from several quarters. The Association of Directors of Social Work offered a thoughtful analysis:

> . . . neighbourhood tensions are on the increase, although the degree of increase appears to vary geographically. However, the lack of a consistent definition of anti-social behaviour makes it difficult to measure the nature of this change.
>
> The term "anti-social behaviour" has come to mean everything from criminal activity such as drug dealing, joy-riding burglaries and racial disputes, through late-night parties, litter and barking dogs, to failure to take a turn at cleaning the stairs. All have the potential to create misery for law-abiding, peaceful and responsible citizens. However, it is essential that distinctions are made between what are essentially very different problems.
>
> The term itself has become largely unhelpful in that it encourages an emotive and over-simplistic response to complex circumstances, sometimes with sensational media coverage. It fails adequately to grasp either the nature of the complaint, or the agency best placed to intervene. It also invites labelling of behaviours that may be culturally or circumstantially determined, rather than a wilful lack of community responsibility. Travelling people, young people and ethnic minorities may be at particular risk of this.

This statement pinpoints the main difficulties facing policy makers seeking to control 'anti-social behaviour':

- Social tensions giving rise to such behaviour are very localised.

- The types of behaviour so-described are disparate in nature and seriousness.

- Different agencies or combinations of agencies may be required to deal with different behaviours.

- The use of one emotive term for such a range of problems encourages simplistic and discriminatory responses.

It would seem that the Scottish Affairs Committee heeded the caution urged upon it by witnesses. Many of its recommendations reflected the powers that were already available to English social landlords under the Housing Act 1996, although it warned against practices such as blanket bans on certain categories of people from joining the waiting list. It sought to tidy up the Scottish law on noise nuisance. In the whole question of neighbour disputes it focussed on better procedures and management; the development of mediation services; and a clearer message to tenants as to what kind of behaviour was unacceptable. The report did not echo the punitive strategies favoured by policy makers south of the border, and did not ask for new forms of criminalisation. As to the definition of 'anti-social behaviour', the Committee considered Shelter's definition (see p.84) quite wide enough.

The weight of Scottish opinion therefore appeared to be against adopting the proposed new legal powers against anti-social behaviour. There was no constitutional or legal necessity for this law to apply in Scotland. But Henry Macleish, the new Minister for Scottish Home Affairs under the Blair government (who had not been a member of the committee) had different ideas. His constituency of Glenrothes had been home to one of the more notorious headline cases of a 'family from hell'. The family concerned were dispatched to wreak their havoc on a small northern fishing village. Mr Macleish insisted that anti-social behaviour orders be available to Scottish local authorities.

The Scottish Office put a brave face on it. It issued a draft circular on 'Housing and Neighbour Problems' in March 1998. This cites both the Shelter definition of 'anti-social behaviour' and the terms set out in the Crime and Disorder Bill. Tactfully it continues:

> Ultimately, it is for landlords to reach their own views on how such behaviour should be defined and categorised. (p.7)

In England and Wales, as shown in the next chapter, it indeed continued to be social landlords who defined the scope of 'anti-social behaviour'. The Social Landlords: Crime and Nuisance Group's survey of members' problems in 1996/7 found that the commonest types were 'noise, garden disputes, criminal behaviour and verbal abuse'. Boundary disputes, vehicle repairs, physical intimidation, harassment, domestic violence and business use of property were also listed. It was indeed beginning to look as though 'anti-social behaviour' was synonymous with almost any management headache caused by tenants short of not paying the rent.

When the anti-social behaviour order finally reached its Parliamentary passage, it received thorough scrutiny only in the House of Lords, where the central problem of definition was highlighted. Lord Goodhart, for the Conservatives,[39] did not oppose in principle but found the threshold much too low for such a powerful order which

> creates a personal criminal law, not a general criminal law. The defendant is not being punished for breaking the law of the land but for breaking a law which applies to him personally.

Guidance provided for implementation of anti-social behaviour orders has attempted to clarify the threshold of what behaviour is or is not to be deemed 'anti-social' enough to merit the new order.[40] But the difficulty of the task is illustrated by the use of phrases such as 'criminal or sub-criminal'. While the order is not advised for 'run-of-the-mill disputes between neighbours', it may be used 'where individuals intimidate neighbours and others through threats or violence or a mixture of unpleasant actions'. So is being anti-social anything from being violent to merely unpleasant? Intention does not have to be proved and it may be hard to do so where intimidation is alleged, for instance:

> . . . where there is persistent unruly behaviour by a small group of individuals on a housing estate or other local area, who may dominate others and use minor damage to property and fear of retaliation, possibly at unsociable hours, as a means of intimidating other people.

Other suggested prototypes for the order include families who turn nasty when their anti-social behaviour is challenged; people who display abusive behaviour towards vulnerable targets such as the elderly or mentally ill, or who harass minority groups; organized serious bullying of schoolchildren; drug or alcohol misusers causing 'persistent anti-social behaviour'.

Those local authorities most likely to want to use ASBOs were presumably the 22 core members of the Social Landlords Crime and Nuisance group (by December 1998 the group also had 88 affiliate members). A handful of keen local authority solicitors working closely with housing management are powering the aggressive use of legislation.[41] But all this legal input has not produced an agreed version

---

39 HOL 3, February 1998, col. 533.
40 Home Office (1999), op. cit.
41 One of the most radical of these is Naseem Malik, who works for Oldham council, and is the author of that authority's stringent new tenancy

of what constitutes anti-social behaviour. The newsletter *Nuisance News* has frequently produced possible definitions but still has no final answer. Despite the caution urged in the Government guidelines, the temptation to 'have a go' at some perceived local unpleasantness of almost any nature is likely to be strong.

This is not to deny the very great difficulties faced by social landlords or to denigrate their efforts. But, to reiterate, it is necessary to to distinguish different types of behaviour with different causation and intent, to draw a clear distinction between what is criminal and what is not, and to avoid policy-making solely from the perspective of one type of agency. This is particularly important as local authorities begin to apply section 1 Crime and Disorder Act 1998. In the run up to implementation, it became clear that a number of housing departments were claiming ownership of the anti-social behaviour order, while other powers were mediated through community safety and youth offending teams (known as 'YOTs'). The reasons for the close involvement of housing management in the legal control of individual behaviour are set out in the next chapter.

---

agreement. When in private practice in Blackburn, she took action against people described as 'neighbours from hell' and says she shares Jack Straw's views on the subject, *Guardian*, 4 March 1998.

CHAPTER 5

The Tools of Tenant Discipline

Policing the poor has become a large part of the role of social housing landlords, at least in areas of the kind described in an earlier chapter. Enormous sums have been spent on estate improvements which, though not primarily undertaken for reasons of safety, have turned out to have a large element of crime control, involving design changes and security devices. New forms of policing have been introduced and social projects have often included the aim of discouraging delinquency and enhancing safety. Management has been recalled from the centre (whither it retreated a few years earlier) and made more localised so as to be able to deal with problems more quickly, including security problems. As has already been indicated in earlier chapters, new-style housing management also involves a closer watch on tenant's behaviour.

David Clapham [1] has pointed out that over the past 20 years the *surveillance* function of housing management has been steadily enhanced and that this is directly related to the changing role of public rented housing. He cites the increased involvement of housing officers in crime prevention programmes; the expectation that they will act in partnership with the police; and the advice they receive about dealing with neighbour disputes and anti-social behaviour. All these roles are now taken for granted but the broader social implications are seldom considered because the work of housing agencies is only researched and analysed in terms of conventional measures of effectiveness, as defined by government. Clapham concludes that:

> In the social context of the concentration of poverty and the problem of criminality in the estates managed by these agencies, this emphasis serves to help sustain the view that the problems of these areas stem from, and can be corrected by, agency action rather than political change . . . [There] is substantial scope for an alternative agenda which places the social construction of housing management within its societal context.

From this perspective it is possible to recognise the legal devices which have been invented to assist the control of tenant's behaviour as essentially the tools of discipline. Although targeted at a presumed minority of 'anti-social' tenants, they involve every tenant in a network of regulation and responsibility, extending not only to herself and the

---

1 D Clapham, 'The Social Construction of Housing Management', *Urban Studies* 34 (1997), 761-774.

immediate family, but to visitors of any description and their activities not just on the premises but in any part of the neighbourhood. Moreover the power to exclude disruptive or potentially dangerous people from access to social housing has been formalised through statutory rules relating to waiting lists and probationary tenancies.

The system relies on two main instruments: the tenancy agreement itself, the details of which may vary from one landlord to another; and the Housing Act 1996, especially Part V ('Conduct of Tenants'). Here statutory force is given to a range of powers used to enforce good behaviour, and existing powers are strengthened in certain important respects. In April 1999 a new power in the Crime and Disorder Act 1998, the anti-social behaviour order, became available, and applies to anybody, not specifically to social tenants.

The main instruments now available to social landlords in terms of controlling tenants' behaviour are therefore as follows.[2] In some circumstances, especially noise nuisance, environmental health powers will also apply: these are discussed in the previous chapter.

- *Access to housing register:* each local authority must keep a register of applicants who are 'qualified' for social housing, but has considerable freedom to decide who does and does not qualify. It may decide that someone does not qualify because of their behaviour or criminal record.

- *Introductory tenancies:* local authorities have the right to adopt a probationary system whereby new tenants have no security of tenure for their first year. Anti-social behaviour may be grounds for refusing a permanent tenancy.

- *Terms of contract:* the tenancy agreement can be used to spell out detailed prohibitions and obligations: breaking the terms of an agreement can be used as grounds for seeking repossession, and/or an injunction.

- *Possession orders:* may be sought in the county court if a tenant has broken the terms of the tenancy agreement or caused a nuisance to neighbours or been convicted of committing/has permitted illegal or immoral activities to take place on the property; or has been convicted of an arrestable offence committed in the dwelling or in the locality. The same prohibitions extend to family and visitors.

---

2 For a fuller account of the legal powers of social landlords with regard to anti-social behaviour, see Caroline Hunter and Kerry Bretherton, *Anti-social Behaviour: Law and Practice in Social Housing* (London, Lemos and Crane, 1998).

- *Injunctions:* there is now a statutory right for local authorities to obtain an injunction against anybody using violence or threat against a tenant or other person (e.g. council staff) going about their lawful business in or near the dwelling, or in discharge of statutory duties towards the homeless, whether or not the landlord's own interest is involved. Power of arrest may be attached. Hearsay evidence is permissible. In urgent cases the injunction can be obtained without first giving notice to the defendant (*ex parte*).

- *Anti-social behaviour order:* established in the Crime and Disorder Act 1998, section 1, and available since April 1999 (see discussion in *Chapter 4*). A civil order backed up with criminal sanctions for breach. Obtainable on application to magistrates by local authority or police against any person over ten years of age (16 years in Scotland) whose conduct might cause 'harassment, alarm or distress' and where the order is necessary to protect people in the local government area from such conduct in future. Breach of the terms of the order (not necessarily a repetition of the conduct itself) constitutes a criminal offence punishable with a maximum of five years' imprisonment (limited to two years detention in a young offender institution for offenders aged 15 to 20 years; or two years secure training for 12 to 14 year olds).

Several of the above powers only became available under the staged introduction of the Housing Act 1996. It is already clear that there are strong regional differences in the extent to which they are being used and enforced.[3] Naturally council landlords vary greatly in the priority and resources accorded to behaviour management. The keenest tend to be those where demand for their housing is weakest. But even in these places, warnings, preliminary notices, and suspended orders may often be all that is required to secure compliance. Courts are not always in agreement with landlords, especially when it comes to evicting a family. So what appears on paper may look more threatening than it is in practice; on the other hand, the threat itself provides an operational tool of considerable force. The fact is that the powers exist, and at least some local authorities are using them with determination—how effectively in the longer run is another unanswered question.

The need for strong legal powers against troublesome tenants did not arise in the days when a council tenancy could be terminated much

---

3 Judy Nixon, Caroline Hunter and Sigrid Shayer, *The Use of Legal Remedies by Social Landlords to Deal with Neighbour Nuisance* (Centre for Economic and Social Research, Sheffield Hallam University, 1999).

more easily. But one of the first actions of the Thatcher government was aimed at over-mighty local government landlords. The Housing Act 1980 (incorporated in the 1985 consolidating Act), through the *Tenants' Charter*, not only gave council tenants the right to buy their homes on very favourable terms, but also gave them, in the form of 'secure tenancies', the sort of legal protection previously only enjoyed by private sector 'protected tenants'. (Ironically, at the same time protection for private tenants was being reduced).

From now on, the law would govern landlord-tenant relations in the public sector in a way that had not previously been thought necessary. This included fixed procedures which had to be observed before anybody was evicted. Eviction of 'secure' council tenants, though not impossible, became considerably harder, since a court order had to be obtained following strict and often lengthy procedures. One or more of the statutory grounds for eviction had to be stated to the court and to the tenant. 'Ground 1' was that the terms of the tenancy agreement had been broken (in practice, most commonly because of failure to pay rent). 'Ground 2'—following private sector practice—was that:

> The tenant or a person residing in the dwelling-house has been guilty of conduct which is a nuisance or annoyance to neighbours, or has been convicted of using the dwelling house or allowing it to be used for immoral or illegal purposes.

This provision was traditionally seen as a means of getting rid of 'problem families' and prostitutes. Only later was it built upon to become an explicit device for crime control, although councils taking a firm anti-racist stance soon started applying it to cases of racial harassment [4].

The development of tenancy agreements

These changes occurred when councils were already taking on a more needy and more vulnerable mix of tenants under the Housing (Homeless Persons) Act 1977. Gradually local authorities started tightening up their tenancy agreements in response to the new legal position, sometimes building in specific prohibitions against harassment of racial and other minority groups. Popplestone's 1979 report[5] had recommended that rules governing tenants' behaviour should be cut to 'a bare minimum' and then better enforced; he had found that managers did not regard it as part of their job to take action against nuisance behaviour and only did so when pressured by 'respectable' tenants and councillors. But in the

---

4 See for example *Islington LBC v Isherwood*, 1987, cit. Susan Bright and Geoff Gilbert, *Landlord and Tenant Law: The Nature of Tenancies* (Oxford, Clarendon Press, 1995), 596.

5 op.cit.

'new politics' of law and order which emerged in the 1990s councils began to adopt new types of detailed control of tenants' behaviour and a more interventionist approach. Redrafting tenancy agreements with the specific aim of discouraging different kinds of anti-social behaviour began to take off, as concern grew at the apparent increase of incidents, and the Housing Act 1996 clarified and strengthened enforcement procedures.

Some councils found that repossession actions failed in court because the behaviour complained of was not necessarily prohibited under the tenancy agreement. This has led to contracts which list examples of behaviour to which prohibitions apply, intended both as a warning and a legal weapon. These are sometimes accompanied by informally worded guidance setting out obligations and rights for tenants.

Model tenancy conditions are recommended to district councils by the (now) Local Government Association, in a paper issued in February 1997 on introductory tenancies.[6] The conditions are copied from Manchester City Council, which pioneered many of the techniques which were endorsed and enhanced in the Housing Act 1996. Tenants' responsibilities in Manchester include the behaviour of every person, including children, living in or visiting the home, both indoors and anywhere in the neighbourhood around the home and examples are given of the kind of things prohibited.

> You, and they, must not cause a nuisance, annoyance or disturbance to any other person. Examples of nuisance, annoyance or disturbance include: loud music; arguing and door slamming; dog barking and fouling; offensive drunkenness; selling drugs or drug abuse; rubbish dumping; playing ball games close to someone else's home'.

> You, and they, must not harass any other person. Examples of harassment include: racist behaviour or language; using or threatening to use violence; using abusive or insulting words or behaviour; damaging or threatening to damage another person's home or possessions; writing threatening, abusive or insulting graffiti; doing anything that interferes with the peace comfort and convenience of other people.

Other clauses specifically forbid 'illegal activities including drug dealing', and domestic violence.

---

6 *Introductory Tenancies: Guidance for Local Authorities.* The Introductory Tenancies Working Group (undated). Of the six local authority representatives on the panel, three were from Manchester and one from Salford, which seems indicative of the strong lead taken by Greater Manchester authorities in matters pertaining to anti-social tenants.

Most people would agree that all the things mentioned here should indeed be avoided for the sake of good neighbourly relations and that most of them are undesirable in themselves. What is remarkable is not the content of the forbidden behaviour, but the fact that the municipal landlord is now so clearly expected to take on the role of 'keeper of the peace', regulator of social relations, and even enforcer of family discipline. The equivalent document issued to tenants by Oldham Metropolitan Borough gives as one of many examples of anti-social behaviour 'not looking after your children properly'.

Some councils take this role still further in the geographical detail of tenancy rules. Coventry's tenants sign up to similar arrangements covering not just the whole of the estate they live on but any place within a mile of it. The agreement is specifically stated to protect neighbours from anti-social behaviour and they are told that 'your neighbours include all *Council tenants in Coventry* [author's italics], everyone living in or working in the area described above, including employees or persons acting on behalf of the Council'. If these conditions were observed to the letter, perfect peace would reign over most of the city.

Rochdale is one of the councils which has been especially active in developing behaviour enforcement. Its tenancy agreement spells out the crime control aspect very explicitly. A clause headed 'Criminal Activity' warns:

> You and/or your household members must not use the property for the sale of illegal drugs, the sale and/or storage of stolen property, storage of unlicensed firearms, prostitution or the use of a property as a brothel, or the illegal alteration of motor vehicles and must not commit burglary, arson, offences relating to joy riding (including driving without a valid licence or insurance), public order offences and offences against the person in the vicinity or neighbourhood of the property.

Illegal activities in or around the home are never going to be uncommon in many neighbourhoods. The question here is how far the municipal landlord is prepared to go to use the power of the possession order, or the threat of it, actually to rid an estate of a household which it knows is involved in some form of crime. The majority of offences most common in poor communities have some kind of link with the area and therefore if proven would be violations of the tenancy. Cases which receive publicity tend to be those where the criminal activity has been of a severely disruptive or aggressive nature.

Eviction
Repossession of council dwellings let to secure tenants may therefore be sought on grounds that some aspect of the tenancy agreement has been

breached, but courts may use their discretion and have to be convinced that the application is reasonable. Repossession under Ground 2— nuisance or criminal conduct—has been widened in Section 144 Housing Act 1996, and procedures speeded up in section 147. Similar controls are provided for landlords of assured tenancies—housing associations—in section 148. A new ground of domestic violence is provided in section 145.

The Act extends the grounds for repossession to include behaviour likely to cause nuisance and to the activities of visitors as well as people living in the house. The behaviour must come under at least one of three categories. It must be 'conduct causing or likely to cause a nuisance or annoyance to a person residing, visiting or otherwise engaged in lawful activity in the locality.' This wide definition of the victim group is repeated in several other sections of the Act. The phrase 'likely to cause' not only means that no actual harm need be proven but also permits evidence by someone other than the victim (such a housing or police officer) who has witnessed the alleged conduct. The other two categories of conduct relate to criminal convictions. As in earlier statutes, the person must have been (i) convicted of using the dwelling or allowing it to be used for 'immoral or illegal purposes'; or (ii) convicted of an arrestable offence committed in, or in the locality of, the dwelling-house. The new detail here is 'in the locality of the dwelling-house', whereas formerly only offences committed within the property were counted for eviction purposes. The offence itself might not involve harming or disturbing neighbours.

Less controversially, Section 145 Housing Act 1996 extends the statutory grounds for repossession specifically to assist the victims of domestic violence. A new 'Ground 2A' can be invoked in a situation where one partner in a domestic couple (married or cohabiting) has left the house and is unlikely to return because of violence to themselves or another member of the family by the other partner. However, this does nothing for the victim unless they have already left the home; and the circumstances may be difficult to prove. It does give some statutory backing to those councils whose policy is to try and maintain the tenancy in favour of a battered partner whilst seeking means to evict the perpetrator, for instance through tenancy clauses prohibiting domestic violence. A House of Lords judgement in July 1998 in favour of Newlon Housing Trust has made it easier for social landlords to do this in the case of joint tenancies.[7] There still needs to be more co-ordination of landlords' use of their powers in domestic violence cases with the further

---

7 [1998] 3 WLR 451; [1998] 4 All ER 1. As the result of this judgement, if an abused partner in a joint tenancy files a notice to quit, the landlord may use discretion in deciding to evict her abuser.

types of court order now available to victims under Part IV of the Family Law Act 1996.

There is no specific repossession ground for social landlords relating to racial harassment but it is generally agreed that this is clearly one type of conduct to be regarded as 'causing a nuisance to neighbours'. It is often made explicit in tenancy agreements and enforcement does take place, although it is not known how many actual evictions have been carried out on these grounds. Reported cases are rare: one example was the eviction of a family whose 16-year-old son was the leader of a racist gang on the Limehouse Fields estate in Tower Hamlets.[8] Bad cases are more likely to be prosecuted now that the Crime and Disorder Act 1998 has introduced a new criminal category of racially aggravated offences.

Eviction/repossession is a slow and costly process which quite often fails in court (see below). But the process involves plenty of scope for compliance in response to warning letters and notices of the intention to seek possession and most people do indeed comply without having to be taken to court. Courts which do grant orders often suspend them, and sometimes this suits the aims of the landlord; there is no information however on the rate of compliance with suspended orders[9]

Eviction as a form of behaviour control raises important questions of principle. One is vicarious punishment: should everybody in a household suffer the loss of their home because of the conduct of perhaps only one member, or even of someone who is only a visitor? The other is double jeopardy: should somebody who has been convicted in the courts and punished by the sentence, be punished again (and other household members, vicariously punished) by having their home repossessed on grounds of that conviction? These are further reasons (cost and time being the main ones) why local authorities have been using alternative enforcement strategies.

Injunctions

Prior to the drafting of the 1996 Act some councils had become particularly concerned about the growth of criminal activity and associated violence on their estates, which stemmed from people who were not themselves tenants. The police seemed unable to stop them, and in these cases tenancy enforcement was irrelevant or inappropriate. New ground was broken in Hackney in 1993. Here, on the Kingsmead estate, the council decided to work jointly with the police in an exercise which brough both civil and criminal powers to bear on a small group of

---

8 *Inside Housing,* 9 April 1998, 2; *Nuisance News,* No 6, June 1998, 10.

9 Caroline Hunter, Tom Mullen and Suzie Scott, *Legal Remedies for Neighbour Nuisance: Comparing Scottish and English Approaches* (York, Joseph Rowntree Foundation, 1998), 25.

youths who were known to have been committing aggressive burglaries and robbery on the estate. Injunctions were used to ban them from entering property and assaulting staff, using affidavits obtained from tenants. The police followed up with a series of arrests. Burglaries and robberies dropped dramatically and it became possible to develop a series of community-building initiatives.[10]

Following Hackney's success the injunction rapidly gained popularity among social landlords as the favoured enforcement option, especially in cases of seriously bad behaviour but also for targeting a range of tenancy breaches. Injunctions can be used in tandem with possession orders but have several advantages over them. They are very much quicker to obtain—sometimes only hours, rather than months. Affidavits may contain hearsay evidence, which may be the only kind obtainable when intimidation is involved. And, because the action is aimed at individuals rather than households it need not involve an innocent tenant—for example the parent of adult children still living at home who could not reasonably be expected to control their conduct. Injunctions, too, carry the potential for a fine or imprisonment of up to two years for contempt of court if the order is disregarded.

Doubts have been raised about the fairness of the procedure. Hunter, Mullen and Scott[11] cite research by Cracknell who looked at one borough which used injunctions systematically from 1993-1995. All were granted, after being heard on unchallenged hearsay evidence in affidavits by a judge in chambers; no defendants, most of whom were single mothers, were represented.

Under the Local Government Act 1972 (section 222) a local authority has a general power to initiate civil proceedings in its own name if it: 'considers it expedient for the promotion or protection of the interests of their [sic] area'. It is this power (not available in Scotland) which has enabled the development of the behaviour restraining injunction against non-tenants (see Finnie, below). It is a power which is not tenure-specific and has been successfully applied to owner occupiers. In Croydon the owner of a flat was creating a nuisance by shouting and playing loud music, and was harassing the occupants of other flats. Environmental Protection Act powers were also used against the noise nuisance. The woman concerned breached the terms of the injunction and in 1997 received a six-month prison committal, suspended for a year.[12]

There is little information on the effectiveness of injunctions in restraining behaviour. Proceedings for breach of an injunction are

---

10 For background and further developments see *Crime, Community and Change: Taking Action on the Kingsmead Estate in Hackney* (London, NACRO, 1996).
11 op. cit. p.30.
12 Hunter and Bretherton, op. cit., 92.

difficult and have to be proven 'beyond reasonable doubt' for punishment to be imposed; imprisonment is rare and very seldom for more than a brief period.[13] A further disadvantage in the eyes of some housing authorities has been that an injunction cannot easily be enforced on anyone under the age of 18—a factor which, as we shall see, has had important implications in terms of the Crime and Disorder Act. This is because only adults can be imprisoned for contempt of court, i.e. for breach of an injunction. The alternative of a fine is seldom realistic for a juvenile.

In Scotland the equivalent power is the 'interdict'. As its name implies it is an instrument for forbidding specified actions; unlike an injunction no positive conditions can be attached. Scottish authorities have not used interdicts as readily as their English counterparts have used injunctions and they are only able to do so where they have 'title and interest'. In the case of *Dundee District Council v Cook* in 1995 the Sheriff held that the local authority had insufficient interest, when neighbours were being bullied by an owner-occupier, to justify their request for an interdict.

Interdicts have similar problems to those of injuctions when breach occurs. As Hunter *et al* explain:

> The difficulties associated with enforcement in both jurisdictions mean that it is precisely the cases where effective enforcement is most needed—where the defendant's behaviour does not improve—that injunction and interdict are likely to be found most wanting.

A high-profile case, which illustrates some important issues, and the difficulties involved, was that of Coventry City Council versus the Finnie brothers. The city obtained *ex parte* interlocutory injunctions in February 1995, banning the two adult brothers from the Stoke Heath estate where their mother was a tenant. They had several convictions and were held to be responsible for burglary, arson and intimidation on the estate. The brothers applied for the injunctions to be lifted and eventually the council were unable to contest the matter, because in order to do so they would have had to produce witnesses in person, and no-one was willing to come forward.[14]

The brothers failed in their subsequent application for damages. It was held, on appeal, that in obtaining an injunction under the Local Government Act 1972 , section 222, Coventry were in this instance acting in a law enforcement capacity. The court accepted that the high level of crime and intimidation, associated with the Finnies, had driven many

---

13 Hunter, Mullen and Scott, op. cit., 32.
14 HOC Standing Committee G, 29 February 1996, col. 432.

tenants from the estate where the family lived, had caused much expense over lost revenues and repairs following burglaries and arson attacks, and had taken up an undue amount of officers' time dealing with complaints. As noted in the report of the case: '[the] criminal law had proved inadequate to protect the lawful interests of the inhabitants of the particular area of Coventry, so the local authority stepped in to invoke the civil law'.[15]

There was a need to clarify the right of local authorities to use their powers under section 222 of the 1972 Act in the context of anti-social behaviour in and around council-owned housing estates—not least because of increasing reports of assaults on their own staff. Section 152 Housing Act 1996 now gives them the right to seek an injunction from the High Court or county court in cases involving threats or violence, if necessary with a power of arrest attached, prohibiting a person from:

(a) engaging or threatening to engage in conduct causing or likely to cause a nuisance or annoyance to a person residing in, visiting or otherwise engaged in lawful activity in residential premises to which this section applies or in the locality of such premises,

(b) using or threatening to use residential premises to which this section aplies for immoral or illegal purposes, or

(c) entering residential premises to which this section applies or being found in the locality of such premises .

[The premises referred to are local authority secure or introductory tenancies or their statutory homeless accomodation].

Furthermore, in section 153, all social landlords, not just local authorities, have stronger powers against aggressive tenants. The power of arrest without warrant may be attached to an injunction in support of an action for breach of tenancy where the tenant's conduct, or anticipated conduct, or that of a lodger or visitor, falls into the categories described above and has been accompanied by violence or the threat of violence. Both clauses have been widely welcomed by housing management as a genuine strengthening of enforcement powers against violence, crime and nuisance.

EXCLUSION FROM SOCIAL HOUSING

So much for the expulsionary powers of the Housing Act 1996. This statute also carries considerable potential for councils to exercise

---

15 29 HLR, Sept/Oct 1997

exclusionary options. These relate to who is granted access to the housing register; who is given priority in allocation; and who is considered well-behaved enough to be eligible for a permanent tenancy.

Potentially the most far-reaching change relating to the issue of tenants' behaviour is contained in section 161 Housing Act 1996, which gives local authorities considerable discretion in deciding who is a 'qualifying person' with regard to allocation of accomodation. No-one who is unqualified can be entered on the 'housing register'. The register, which the Act states must be maintained by the local authority, is a single list of all those applying for housing and is the source of access both to council tenancies or (increasingly) to alternative forms of social rented housing including housing associations. Not only do local authorities have nomination rights to a large slice of housing association tenancies (and are often accused of 'dumping' problem tenants on them), but many areas now operate a common list covering all social housing. The register replaces all other forms of housing list formerly kept by a local authority, although the change does not affect the statutory right of homeless people to appear on the housing register.

The only specific rule in section 161 concerning qualification states that asylum seekers (the latest addition to the canon of unwelcome strangers) shall not be qualifying persons. But otherwise local authorities, whilst still having to have regard to housing need, can make most of their own rules about who qualifies for acceptance on to the housing register and what details are included on the register (section 161(4)). This leaves them free to rule out individuals or classes of persons or to append information to an entry which might result in an application being effectively moth-balled. They may also remove (or suspend) someone from their housing register who has not asked to be so removed 'in such circumstances as they think fit' (subject to notification and review). These provisions leave wide scope for excluding from access to social housing difficult or controversial persons (they have been widely used against sex offenders for example). Someone moving into the area who is known to have been thrown out elsewhere for bad behaviour may find themselves black-balled. (For further discussion of this issue see *Chapter 6*).

Introductory tenancies
As another bulwark against the possibility of being saddled with difficult tenants who are hard to remove, Part V of the Housing Act 1996 gives local authorities the option of operating 'introductory tenancies', whereby a new tenant does not become secure straight away but has a year's trial period, during which time if his or her conduct has not been good enough he or she will not be allowed to remain. (The same system

does not apply to tenants of housing associations since they never have the same degree of security of tenure, but Housing Action Trusts may use the introductory system). If a landlord applies for a possession order at the end of an introductory tenancy the county court must oblige, provided that specified procedures have been observed, including setting out the reasons for applying for the order. The tenant can seek a review, but only within 14 days from notice of proceedings being served, and it is the local authority itself which conducts the review and its decision is final, subject only to judicial review on grounds of natural justice.[16]

Among the criticisms levelled at this idea is the implication that new tenants are more likely to be a source of trouble than existing ones. Given the suspicion with which some communities regard newcomers, there is also the possibility of scapegoating. Local authorities are supposed to be vigilant against discriminatory complaints. The Act does not state the kind of reasons which would be valid grounds for ending an introductory tenancy but it is clear from the context this is intended as yet another device to control anti-social behaviour. Guidelines on introductory tenancies from the Local Government Association[17] do attempt to distinguish degrees of 'anti-social' conduct which would justify the refusal of a secure tenancy: for instance minor breaches like occasional noise or littering should not count; violence, threats, persistent minor harassment seriously detrimental to the victim should prompt a notice of repossession.

By January 1999, according to a survey by Sheffield Hallam University[18] 30 per cent of local authorities said that they were using introductory tenancies, and 12 per cent more were about to introduce them, with a strong concentration in the north-east of England. Councils are divided: an earlier survey by the Social Landlords' Crime and Nuisance Group found that over 45 per cent of respondents said that they had decided against introductory tenancies, either because they saw no need for them or felt that they were unfair. As yet no evaluation of their effectiveness as a deterrent against anti-social behaviour has been carried out.

Anti-social behaviour orders

A new and controversial instrument of controlling individual behaviour —anywhere in a local authority area, not merely on council estates—is provided in section 1 of the 1998 Act, which became operational in April 1999. This is the 'anti-social behaviour order', which can be made against

---

16 See the issues raised in City of *Manchester v Cochrane*, p.115 below.

17 op. cit., 9.

18 Nixon, Hunter and Shayer, op cit.

anyone over the age of ten behaving in an 'anti-social' manner, defined in section 1(1)(a) as 'a manner that caused or was likely to cause harassment, alarm or distress to one or more persons not of the same household as himself'. The order must be necessary to protect people in the local authority area from further anti-social conduct. It is obtained only on the request of the local authority or the police (who must consult jointly) through application to a magistrates' court acting in a civil capacity. It is in the form of an injunction, lasting at least two years, setting out any negative conditions thought necessary to achieve the required protection. Although it is a civil order, any breach (without reasonable excuse) is criminal offence, punishable by a maximum of five years custody—this compares with a two year maximum for breach of an ordinary civil injunction. This sanction applies even if the the original bad conduct would attract a much lower penalty, or none if no crime is involved (although it might be only the rare case that would reach the Crown Court and be liable for the maximum penalty).

The order has attracted exceptional opposition from legal experts and civil liberties groups. When the preceding consultation paper was issued by the government[19]—at this stage the order was still described as the 'Community Safety Order'—six law professors joined in a detailed condemnation of its terms and implications.[20] Their main criticisms were directed at (a) its imprecise and sweeping scope, which could effectively criminalise merely unpopular behaviour; (b) the low standards of proof and violations of due process, almost certainly in contravention of the Human Rights Act 1998; (c) the disproportionate nature of the penalties. Some of these issues will be considered further in the final chapter.

A further line of criticism is that no convincing case was ever made out for the necessity of such an innovation. As far as children are concerned, persistent behaviour sufficient to cause distress etc. to neighbours suggests that the Family Proceedings Court should intervene. For adults, criminal prosecution on the one hand and straightforward civil injunctions on the other, if effectively pursued, should cover any conduct forseeably relevant, especially in view of the wide application of section 222 Local Government Act 1972. Police co-operation in providing evidence for local authorities to use in civil cases was already established procedure in some cities.[21] The original Labour party proposal (see pp. 87-88) made much of the difficulty of obtaining convictions especially in view of widespread witness intimidation in the

---

19 Home Office (1997), op. cit.
20 Andrew Ashworth, John Gardner, Rod Morgan, ATH Smith, Andrew von Hirsch, Martin Wasik, 'Neighbouring on the Oppressive: The Government's "Community Safety Order" Proposals', *Criminal Justice*, 16.1 (1998), 7-14.
21 Sheridan Morris, op. cit.

kind of scenarios described. This was the fundamental reason for lowering the standard of proof to that of civil law ('balance of probabilities) and allowing hearsay evidence as in civil injunctions. But the ASBO, apart from permitting the use of professional witnesses, does nothing extra to protect victims or other potential witnesses when it comes to enforcement which requires evidence to be upheld to the criminal standard of proof. (On the issue of witness protection, see p.127)

After the enactment of the Crime and Disorder Act a stream of official guidance on implementation of the various aspects issued from the Home Office. Following lengthy consultation, the guidance on the anti-social behaviour order [22] emerged in noticeably tougher form (especially against young people) than the original draft. ASBOs are said to be intended to cover 'criminal or sub-criminal activity which, for one reason or another, cannot be proven to the criminal standard, or where criminal proceedings are not appropriate'. But they 'are not intended to replace existing criminal offences, for instance in the Public Order Act 1986, but there may be circumstances when they provide an alternative means of dealing with such behaviour.' The guidelines urge care against discriminatory actions; emphasise the wide consultation across agencies when action is contemplated; and list the many alternative ways of dealing with anti-social behaviour, including mediation. But the authorities are not obliged to exhaust other possibilities before seeking an ASBO.

Many local authorities which pressed for such an order did so largely because they regretted their inability to bring injunctions against under-18s and saw this as a means of filling the gap. Through the guidance document, and its presentation by the Home Secretary Jack Straw, they were clearly given the go-ahead to use the new order freely against 12 to 17 year-olds, although more circumspectly for children of ten and eleven, who may however receive orders if involved in bad behaviour with adults (for instance where whole families are regarded as 'anti-social').

Other measures in the Crime and Disorder Act, notably child curfews, are relevant to the management of behaviour by social landlords, and like ASBOs can apply in any context, regardless of tenure. South Lanarkshire, which pioneered a similar system in three estates in Hamilton, in 1999 extended its 'Child Safety Initiative' to the whole town.

---

22 Home Office (1999), op. cit.

THE USE OF LEGAL POWERS BY LOCAL AUTHORITIES

The most recent survey information about how social landlords are using the new powers granted in the Housing Act 1996, and other legal powers, to control the behaviour of their tenants, provides strong indications that the practice is growing.[23] At the time of writing the local crime and disorder strategies which are obligatory under the Crime and Disorder Act 1998 had barely begun to take shape, and would certainly be expected to bring a different perspective to the issues involved. Nixon *et al* point out that the poor recording systems of most social landlords mean that accurate information on complaints and enforcement is scarce. There are no official sources other than not-very-informative statistics on possession orders published by the Lord Chancellor's Office. Reported cases involving challenges to the 1996 Act have barely emerged, though some cases relating to the Housing Act 1996 are also relevant. There has also been a scattering of press reports on alleged social effects of enforcement.

Pre-1996 Act Surveys
As indicated in the previous chapter, the subject of neighbour nuisance and anti-social behaviour related to housing has had much more extensive consideration in Scotland, from both academic and government sources[24] In 1995 a comprehensive survey of housing management[25] looked at neighbour nuisance along with a whole range of issues, but found less concern among managers about neighbour problems than about people keeping pets and livestock. Respondents viewed most complaints as trivial and showing lack of tolerance; serious nuisance was rare and only 19 per cent of authorities said that they would seek an eviction on these grounds. Even so, dealing with complaints took up about 20 per cent of their time and the same

---

23 Surveys being completed in 1999 by Glasgow University for the Scottish Office and Sheffield Hallam University for the Joseph Rowntree Foundation provide the first general picture. First stage findings suggest growing use of legal powers to control the behaviour of social tenants and confirm the existence of strong regional differences, with the most active authorities in the north of England and a quite different pattern in London as compared with other Metropolitan areas. Nixon, Hunter and Shayer, op cit.

24 For a Scottish overview and bibliography, see *Housing and Neighbour Problems*, Draft Circular, Scottish Office Development Department, March 1998.

25 David Clapham *et al*, op cit. This study consisted of a postal survey of all public housing landlords, case studies of nine of them, a household survey of 2,226 tenants and tenant discussion groups.

proportion of tenants said that they had experienced a problem in the past year, with noise predictably by far the most common.

The Scottish Affairs Committee took extensive evidence on housing and anti-social behaviour before producing its report in December 1996 (discussed in the previous chapter). Following this the Scottish Office Development Department drafted guidance to landlords on good practice, which confined the definition of anti-social behaviour to that which 'threatens the physical or mental health, safety or security of other households or individuals'. Changes to Scottish law have paralleled the English Crime and Disorder Act provisions up to a point, but there are significant differences—for example the police are not involved in applying for anti-social behaviour orders (though the chief constable must be consulted) and the order's bottom age limit is 16 instead of ten as in England and Wales. Moreover there is no framework for local crime and disorder strategies or statutory crime prevention partnerships within which to exercise the new powers, which altogether seem to carry a lower profile in Scotland.

The NACRO survey on English local authority action against neighbour nuisance[26] arose out of the Brixton tenants' survey described in an earlier chapter (pp.60-61). The sample of 125 local authorities who replied, mainly revealed how little they really knew about or responded to nuisance/anti-social behaviour. However it was clearly a significant issue for the 15 per cent of authorities who were spending over £100,000 per year on the consequences. At this stage many authorities were only in the process of developing policies and procedures—for instance only half had formal systems for recording complaints. Predictably, the majority of complaints were about noise, so it was perhaps surprising that only 53 per cent of authorities said that the Environmental Protection Act 1990 was one of the methods used. By far the most popular option (82 per cent) was possession/eviction procedure, although it is not stated how often only the preliminary stages, short of court action, were involved. Injunctions were used by 59 per cent. Only 38 per cent used mediation services. There was no clear indication of what was the most effective method. NACRO recommended that there should be guidelines for monitoring and preventing anti-social behaviour, and procedures to prevent inappropriate court action.

The survey of 20 members of the Social Landlords Crime and Nuisance Group[27] not surprisingly showed much more consciousness of

---

26 F Warburton, M Liddle and J Smith, *Nuisance and Anti-Social Behaviour: A Report of a Survey of Local Authority Housing Departments.* (London, NACRO, 1997). The postal survey was conducted in February-April 1996, so that powers in the Housing Act 1996 would not yet have been available.

27 op. cit, 1998.

the problem and a more proactive approach. In contrast to the more representative group surveyed by NACRO, these landlords were more likely to use injunctions rather than possession proceedings (170 cases compared with 129 in the 12 months April 1996 to March 1997) and were much more likely to get what they wanted from the courts with injunctions—a 95 per cent success rate compared with 66 per cent for possession orders.

Injunctions are used frequently by the most proactive landlords while others never or rarely use them.[28] The example of Manchester City Council, which has a dedicated 'Neighbour Nuisance Strategy Team' within its housing department, show a steep rise in legal action against tenants on grounds of 'nuisance' issues from 1996, with the bulk of the increase in the form of injunctions, which more than doubled in 1998 compared with the previous year. Injunctions may, of course, be the preliminary to further actions. Two hundred and thirty actions for nuisance behaviour in 1998 may not seem great among Manchester's 76,000 tenancies, especially as some tenants will have been subject to more than one type of action, but this compares with 44 in 1995 and a mere eight in 1992. In 1998 the availability of injunctions with power of arrest attached meant that the city obtained 66 of these within a total of 164 injunctions against tenants. Six people were sent direct to prison for breaching injunctions and 15 were subject to exclusion orders.

Table 2: Manchester City Council: Legal Actions by Neighbour Nuisance Strategy Team.

	Injunction (power of arrest)	Committal (suspended)	Possessions	Eviction/ Immediate possession	Exclusion orders	Total legal actions p.a.
1992	7		1	1		8
1993	30	4 (2)	13	10		47
1994	22	4	3	2		31
1995	28	2	14	9		44
1996	79	6	12	8		97
1997	77 (1)	7	15	14	6	105
1998	164 (66)	19 (13)	32	27	15	230
TOTAL	407	42	90	71	21	

Author's note: figures do not include repossession of introductory tenancies. Evictions are not separate legal actions, being simply enforced as possession orders, and therefore do not count towards the annual totals of legal actions.

---

28 Nixon *et al*, op. cit.

JUDICIAL ACTION.

Respondents to the Social Landlords Group survey reflected the dissatisfaction with judicial attitudes which is frequently encountered among local government housing spokespeople, although it is not entirely obvious why they should feel that way, given that actions against nuisance behaviour are much more likely to succeed than repossessions for rent arrears.[29] In the respondents' view, judges' understanding of housing issues was rated at only 69 per cent for possession orders and 64 per cent for injunctions, despite their almost total success in obtaining the latter. The same message was sent very strongly to Lord Woolf at the time of his inquiry into civil justice[30] and he was taken on a tour of some of the worst afflicted estates in Manchester. Although social landlords have a scarcely impartial view of judgements that go against them, it must also be true that the intensity of the misery that the worst sorts of behaviour can inflict on a neighbourhood are barely imaginable to anyone, not only a judge, whose life is untouched by the experience.

Lord Woolf responded by acknowledging the very serious consequences of the worst kinds of harassment and nuisance, including witness intimidation (p.207). He went on to say: 'I am particularly disturbed by reports that courts do not recognise the special significance of these cases and consequently fail to treat them with the appropriate degree of urgency'. He recommended speeded up procedures in such cases and the introduction of specialist housing judges who 'should regard it as their duty to visit local council estates and hold structured discussions with tenants representatives' (p.208).

The only statistical series in this field to be found is *Judicial Statistics*, published by the Lord Chancellor's office, under 'Social Landlords: Possession Actions Other Than Mortgages'. There is no indication of the different grounds involved, but in 1997 the number of actions entered by social landlords, 107,861, was higher than at any time since the series began in 1990, although the total number of orders made was comparable with earlier years (82,207, of which 64,147 were suspended). Recent years have seen a growth in the proportion of orders which are suspended, but how far these relate to rent arrears and how far to other matters is unknown. If the statistics from the Lord Chancellor's office

---

29 Nixon *et al*, op. cit.
30 *Access to Justice: Final Report to the Lord Chancellor on the Civil Justice System in England and Wales*, The Right Honourable the Lord Woolf, Master of the Rolls (London, HMSO, 1996).

could include a breakdown of the grounds for possession, this would be helpful in tracing future developments.

Legal challenges

An obvious area of challenge to enforcement proceedings is the meaning of 'the locality' which is a term used in the Housing Act 1996 to extend control of prohibited behaviour beyond the limits of the tenanted property itself. A similar challenge was raised in respect of the definition of 'neighbour' in an appeal heard in November 1997. *Northampton Borough Council v Lovatt* related to a Ground 2 possession action under the Housing Act 1985.[31] The issue was whether anti-social and criminal activities carried out by the tenant's sons over 100 yards from the dwelling could count as nuisance and annoyance to neighbours; the court decided that it could.[32]

At the committee stage of the Housing Bill the Minister, David Curry, explained that the term 'locality' had been chosen in preference to 'vicinity' or 'neighbourhood' because the Government wanted the area covered in prevention of anti-social behaviour to be as wide as possible.[33] But how wide is 'wide'? When Mrs Lawler, a tenant of Manchester City Council, was said to have breached her tenancy by reason of aggressive behaviour, she was placed under an injunction not to 'cause a nuisance, annoyance or disturbance to anybody' in 'the locality' of her address. She subsequently threatened a child with a knife in a nearby shopping street. When breach proceedings were brought the judge said that there should have been a more precise definition of 'locality'. On appeal, however, it was held that 'locality' in section 152 Housing Act 1996 could not be defined by distance or street names. Sometimes the meaning would be obvious, sometimes less so. 'In each case it will be a question of fact for the judge whether the place in which the conduct occurred was or was not within the locality'.[34] This judgement suggests that many more legal arguments about 'the locality' will arise in particular cases.

---

31 30 HLR 875.

32 Some press reports have highlighted the pressures on tenants when the behaviour of family members brings the danger of eviction. In Halifax a woman with three children was reported as saying that she was going to divorce her husband who had been convicted of cannabis-dealing from the home; the tenancy was in her name and otherwise she would have lost it, *Halifax Courier*, 12 August 1998. Parents in Sunderland were said to be putting children into care (or refusing to have them back) rather than risk losing the family home as a result of the children's criminal behaviour, *Guardian* 8 June 1998; *Inside Housing*, 12 June 1998; *The Economist*, 11 July 1998.

33 HOC Standing Committee G, 27 February 1996.

34 *Manchester City Council v Lawler* (1998), cit. Hunter and Bretherton, 58-59.

Over and above the validity of reasons for eviction, wider procedural questions have been raised concerning the method of challenge to the decision to repossess from an introductory tenant (HA96, section 129). *Manchester City Council v Cochrane*[35] confirmed that, provided the local authority has followed correctly the procedures laid down in the Act, the county court has no discretion but must grant repossession. If the tenant wants to challenge the local authority's decision on grounds of natural justice or other considerations of public law, that is a matter for judicial review. The private-public law interface of local authority tenancy regulation is disputed territory which this book has no scope to explore, other than to recognise it as in effect another source of burden on tenants, given the length and difficulty of the process of judicial review.

INFORMATION SHARING

Social landlords cannot evict a tenant on grounds of criminal activity or a conviction unless they have clear evidence of the same, and they may wish for similar information about new applicants. This means information of a kind which they do not automatically possess. Housing managers have grassrooots contacts; verbal tip-offs from local constables have long been available in some localities. Some authorities scan court reports in the local press. Increasingly, however, local protocols (sometimes known as 'safer estate agreements')[36] are being agreed for obtaining information from the police in a manner which does not breach the Data Protection Act 1998 (which anyway in section 29 exempts information relating to crime prevention, detection and prosecution). For instance it would be acceptable for the police to tell the housing department about who is appearing in court, which is anyway in the public domain. The department can then find out the result of the case and obtain a certificate of conviction from the court. Some police forces agree to supply information on incidents, arrests and charges, as well as convictions, in order to support civil cases brought by the local authority, and allow officers to give evidence in civil cases.[37] Detailed sharing of information on problem tenants can help both agencies in their task, and 'bad' families held under intensive surveillance, sometimes by use of video cameras and other covert means, may just disappear from an estate. But in one example quoted by Morris (Kingsmead, Hackney) where this happened, another criminal family

---

35 Case unreported at time of writing.   `\`
36 Nixon *et al*, op. cit. found that 71 per cent of local authorities had information sharing arrangments with the police, as did half of other social landlords.
37 Sheridan Morris, op.cit.

surfaced once the original gang had gone, and this is unlikely to be an unusual occurrence.

The joint working which now takes place under the duty of co-operation with police and other responsible bodies (Crime and Disorder Act 1998, section 5) will facilitate such arrangements; for example by making quite clear the addresses to which police have frequently been called, or where drug dealing is taking place. Section 115 (disclosure of information) permits disclosure of restricted information to a 'relevant authority' (police chief, local authority, probation committee, health authority) 'where the disclosure is necessary or expedient for the purposes of any provision of this Act'. It does not therefore apply to Housing Acts except where the functions overlap. But a model agreement on joint working produced by the Social Landlords Crime and Nuisance Group, Crime Concern and two Midlands police forces provides for co-ordinated case management, which includes agreeing on whether a criminal or civil route should be taken.

The spread of disclosure is in tune with other recent legislation, such as the Police Act 1995 which permits disclosure of past convictions to employers. Where public safety is genuinely at risk, or when it is quite clear that neighbours require urgent relief from the depredations of a handful of individuals, there can be few qualms.[38] But not all crime by neighbours is of a predatory nature. Is it acceptable that a landlord should know all about the arrest or even conviction of a tenant for, say, storing stolen goods, when the consequence could be the loss of a family home?

Information sharing between landlords is also widespread and has serious implications, as discussed later in this chapter.

Use of electronic surveillance

To these measures must be added the physical surveillance provided by CCTV—now commonplace in many semi-public settings, employed in some degree by almost all the 20 landlords in the group survey mentioned above. This will usually be to guard 'hot-spots' or as additional entry-security. Video surveillance may be installed temporarily to obtain evidence of persistent anti-social behaviour in a specific case. Yet the same survey found only eight cases stemming from

---

38 A Newcastle housing association which had housed 'major players in the criminal fraternity in the west end of Newcastle' (known for its violence and intimidation) sponsored two police officers to work on the estate and had police checks run on applicants (to which they had to agree). As a result one third of would-be tenants were rejected, and crime was said to have dropped by 86 per cent, *Inside Housing*, 8 May 1998, 5.

the use of CCTV; although this finding might not include cases where CCTV provided useful additional evidence.

Professional witnesses and witness protection

Much has been made of the use of professional witnesses in arguments on both sides of the libertarian divide.[39] There are two senses in which this term applies. One is that of a professional person such as a policeman or housing officer who has evidence acquired in the course of their normal work. The other is the employment of private investigators to obtain evidence. Despite the expense of the latter, 35 per cent of councils and 29 per cent of other social landlords say they have used them.[40] The usual use is to obtain evidence of nuisance behaviour which would justify eviction. Some local authorities use their own investigators to obtain evidence of criminal activity, for instance by installing a 'tenant' in the house next door to suspected drug dealers. A less-than happy outcome was reported from Greenwich where the council spent £7,000 on a team of hired investigators who produced no evidence, but were revealed on video playing poker instead of watching.[41]

Quite soon the limitations of the 'planted' witness began to be understood. In physical terms there is not always a conveniently sited vantage point with good vision of suspicious activity. If the offending behaviour consists of a number of small incidents over a long period the watching period required may simply be too long and too expensive; if it is spread out geographically there is no point in a fixed viewing location.[42] Especially in view of the cost, it is likely to be reserved in future for very specific circumstances and serious cases.

Witness intimidation, the problem which gives rise to the need for third-party witnesses, was brought a small step nearer control in late 1998 when Manchester City Council successfully persuaded the Court of Appeal to overturn a county court ruling that it could only deal with witness intimidation that took place in or near the court building. The incident in this case took place when the witness arrived home after giving prosecution evidence. But if it had not been directly associated with his return from court it would not have been possible for the county court to treat it as contempt.[43] Local authorities would like the new witness protection measures being introduced into criminal courts in the Youth Justice and Criminal Evidence Act 1999 to be extended to civil

---

39   Andrew Ashworth *et al*, op.cit. refer to 'the "professional witnesses" which the scheme (amazingly) also contemplates'.

40   Nixon *et al*, op.cit.

41   *Inside Housing*, 24 January1996.

42   *Speaking Up For Justice*, 123.

43   *Inside Housing*, 4 December 1998.

cases where witnesses are vulnerable, if necessary transferring them to criminal courtrooms where the necessary facilities of video link etc are available.

RESTRICTING ACCESS TO HOUSING

The power to disqualify applications for social housing to individuals or classes of persons on grounds of their past or possible future behaviour is the first really hot issue to have arisen from the Housing Act 1996, in conjunction especially with the new restrictions on sex offenders in the Crime and Disorder Act 1998. Although certain types of sex offenders clearly pose the most sensitive rehousing issues, the blanket bans declared on this group by some local housing authorities are not seen as helpful, since they will make supervision in the community more difficult and thus increase rather than reduce risk.[44] And if sex offenders should not be banned, can any general ban based on offence-type be justified? All official guidance, including that of the professional body the Chartered Institute of Housing, is against blanket bans; and the rules which apply if specific groups of people are excluded from the register are tightly drawn, allowing no exceptions once a category is defined. Many councils which initially considered banning whole classes of offenders from their estates have shied away from doing so.

Instead, many local authorities are adopting rules which will have much the same effect. Rather than pronouncing blanket policies, which permit no discretion, they may arrange through the police to investigate applicants for past convictions, or require people to declare unspent convictions for certain offences on their application form. A subsequent discovery of a false statement may result in eviction. People with serious crimes (however defined) in their past may have to ask probation officers to declare them 'safe'. There is an appeal against exclusion from the register available in section 164, but only to the local authority itself. The Local Government Ombudsman has sometimes found procedures unfair: for example a man who was excluded from the register in South Tyneside had not been told that his convictions would be checked.[45] In another case in this borough, the council's officers were found to have prepared misleading reports about an applicant.

All this is with the intention of protecting existing tenants and reducing management problems, but may effectively make it impossible

---

44 Chartered Institute of Housing, *Rehousing Sex Offenders: A Summary of the Legal and Operational Issues* (Coventry, CIH, 1998). See also NACRO, *Sex Offenders: Reducing the Risk* (London, NACRO, 1998).

45 *Legal Action*, August 1998, 21.

to rehouse large numbers of people, especially where any degree of Class A drug dealing has been known. This does not, of course, guarantee that former drug-dealers will not turn up as residents in areas of social housing—perhaps as owner-occupiers in mixed-tenure estates; or sharing a dwelling with an existing tenant. If they are successfully barred from council-owned property, offenders are increasingly likely to become concentrated with other social landlords, or private landlords, who are less well equipped to deal with problem tenants.

People who have been evicted for anti-social or criminal conduct; or who are known for such behaviour, may well find themselves counted as unqualified for a tenancy in their home area; or if placed on the register will be kept forever at the back of the queue (housing managers will sometimes privately admit to the latter ploy). The increasing use of common waiting lists, shared by all social landlords in an area, and a growing network of shared information among different district councils and housing associations may mean that they find themselves unable to obtain any social housing at all. There are many parts of the country where people barred from social housing will be able to obtain private lodgings; but there are also many areas and circumstances (especially for under-25s, who have reduced eligibility for housing benefit) where this will not be possible. In one area known to the author, where housing association tenants were greatly troubled by 'problem' tenants in neighbouring private lodgings, the association took the initiative in offering 'good' private landlords access to joint information on people who should not be housed.

It is local authorities in the Midlands and North which are most likely to use exclusion lists, again reflecting the difference in these housing markets compared with London, where exclusion is less common. Registered social landlords (housing associations and others) are even more likely to operate exclusion of 'nuisance neighbours' in these regions.[46]

The potential scale of the exclusion mechanism is illustrated by the fact that in early 1999 Manchester City housing department had around 11,000 names on what it called the 'under review' list.[47] These were people who, at least temporarily, were banned from council housing for a variety of reasons, including past rent arrears as well as bad behaviour. (At this time the 'under review' policy was itself being reviewed).

Once blacklisted by a local authority for reasons of anti-social behaviour, names are frequently passed on to other local authorities, to social landlords in the same area and, in a significant minority of local

---

46 Nixon *et al,* op. cit., pp.55 -57.
47 Personal information.

authorities, to private landlords as well.[48] People with bad names may therefore be totally excluded from renting across whole districts, except from landlords with similar reputations. As Nixon *et al* comment (p.57) 'In the light of [the] lack of information about the operation and criteria used in exclusion policies, it is of concern that the majority of landlords operating such policies shared information about excluded households with other landlords'

The continued duty to house homeless people in need causes concern among local authorities who do not want to find that they have rehoused somebody expelled from another part of the country for bad behaviour. Government guidance on the allocation of accomodation to homeless people under the Housing Act 1996 reveals the dilemma. The Code of Practice[49] acknowledges that a local authority may choose to disqualify certain classes of people from the waiting list. 'Such groups might include people with a history of anti-social behaviour, people who have attacked housing department staff, or tenants with a record of rent arrears'.(para. 4.27). At the end of the Code, a checklist is presented of the types of need which might be considered as criteria for rehousing. These include for example people living in hostels; people leaving institutional care; facing eviction or repossession; suffering from a mental disorder or disability; young people at risk; people with behavioural difficulties. How is a local authority performing its social duty towards groups like these going to avoid individuals who annoy neighbours, commit crimes, or have a record of offending?

However, despite all these precautions, early indications that bad conduct is unlikely to be the core issue that the new system might imply is gained from a review by Shelter[50] of exclusions from housing registers in the years 1996/7 and 1997/8. Their survey found that exclusions and suspensions had increased nearly fourfold in the second year. Altogether the responding authorities had excluded or suspended 32,971 households in this period: extrapolated to the whole of England this would represent a figure of nearly 200,000. The more recent figure from Manchester cited above suggests that now the figure would be even larger. But the commonest reason for exclusion found by Shelter was for rent arrears, and anti-social behaviour was given as the ground in only three per cent of cases. Other excluded people included squatters, travellers and people who had abandoned housing or left it in a poor state. Those who were excluded for reasons of behaviour were

48 Nixon *et al,* op. cit. p 58.
49 Department of the Environment, *Code of Guidance on Parts VI and VII of the Housing Act 1996. Allocation of Housing Accomodation: Homelessness.* (London, December 1996).
50 Sophie Butler, ed. Nicola Bacon, *Access Denied* (London, Shelter, June 1998).

sometimes being punished vicariously—because of the actions of others in the house. One example cited by Shelter was of a woman who had formerly been living with the son of a family in his parents' house; the family were evicted for neighbour nuisance and she was also put on the exclusions list, although she was not involved in the conduct and had since left her former partner.

Exclusion as property rescue

The authorities most prone to use the tool of exclusion are those in the north east and the north west of England.[51] It is increasingly clear that the most zealous action takes place where the social housing market is weakest and landlords are struggling to fill unwanted properties. It is easy for exclusion to become part of the desperate attempt of housing managers in these areas to make their properties more attractive and their rent rolls more viable. This means, among other things, excluding people seen as likely to render their task still harder, either because they may behave in a way which might put off other people or because they are bad risks financially. Yet the aim may be overridden by the urgency of filling empty properties with anybody willing to occupy them. This is the modern form of the recurring tension between housing need and management criteria, which produces both pressure and counter-pressure for tighter controls over the conduct and life-styles of social housing tenants.

Calderdale in West Yorkshire is a case in point. Tenants are being tempted back to an unpopular estate with offers of curtains, carpets, security devices and garden planting—the more unpopular the property, the more the goodies. The deal is that :

> [New] tenants will have to agree to be vetted. Anyone with unspent convictions for burglary, violence, or sex and drug offences will not be allowed to move to the estate. They will also be checked for past incidents of anti-social behaviour. . . . Residents' Association Chair Heather Terry said the group had pressed for the new policy. "Things have to change for the better. If you get nuisance people moving in others will move away" she said.[52]

This arrangement can be seen as the new version of old-fashioned management practices which were designed to separate 'respectable' and 'rough' tenants.

---

51 Butler and Bacon, op. cit., confirmed by Nixon, Hunter and Shayer's more recent survey.

52 *Inside Housing,* 6 November 1998, 7.

Allocations—deciding who lives where—has always been the key to the differing character of different housing areas and to a large extent this has been a self-selecting process. The growth of tenant co-operatives and other mechanisms for power-sharing with tenants is one way of re-establishing social order in estates which lack that element. Opening up the allocation process to encourage family networks or other groups of people who want to live together has been found to be an effective way of 'rebuilding communities', to use a much-vaunted concept. There is so much that is positive about initiatives of this kind that it seems almost mean to raise caveats. But the effect in relation to the excluded groups in society—who also need to live somewhere—is something which has to be considered.[53] In conclusion we will look at this issue along with other wider implications of the policies described in the present chapter.

---

53 One example is in a small development by the Manningham Housing Association in Bradford. Tenants were chosen on the basis of friendship, family, and pledges of 'mutual aid' rather than housing need. Bradford City Council is said to be interested in the project as a blueprint for tackling 'social exclusion', but at the same time concerned that it could spell literal exclusion for homeless people and those who need support but cannot offer anything in return. The association claims to be flexible: *Inside Housing*, 25 September 1998.

CHAPTER 6

Banishment or Inclusion?

In recent years social landlords have acquired an extraordinary degree of legal control over the behaviour of tenants and their families. The crime-preventive features of tenancy agreements and accompanying statute law echo the disease-preventing regulations applied to working-class tenants a hundred years ago. While it is true that most of the time the control is not actively exercised, it is nevertheless the case that people who enter into an agreement to become the tenant of a local authority, a housing association or one of the growing number of tenant-run estates will in varying degrees be placing themselves in a position where their past, present or possible future behaviour, and that of all household members, may be subject to scrutiny and may be used to deprive them of their home or even to bar them from further tenancies in the social sector. It is hard to think of any other group of adult citizens, outside institutional life, subject to the same level of governance in their daily lives.

It is a trend which stigmatises all tenants, good and bad, alike; and which, at a time when local democracy is considered at a low point, has greatly enhanced the bureaucratic arm of the local state. Legal actions and administrative barriers introduced by social landlords, taken together with the enhanced policing functions of local authorities created by the Crime and Disorder Act 1998, are intended to be seen as forms of protection for honest citizens, although risking serious infringement of individual and family rights. Sooner or later they are bound in one way or another to fall foul of the European Convention On Human Rights.

It could be argued that these intrusions are not really significant because most people potentially affected are scarcely aware of the rules and a random tour of estates would make it obvious that they are flouted daily. But the whole reason for the new prohibitions and powers directed at criminal and 'nuisance' behaviour was because these things were seen to be growing out of hand in many impoverished neighbourhoods. The more that tenants complained, or voted with their feet, the more the answer was seen to lie in stronger powers for landlords, more prohibitions written into tenancy agreements, and tougher enforcement. From the perspective of the local authority housing departments—and it was a few powerful ones which led the way—it made sense to exploit their position as property owners and use their rights in civil law as the means to reimpose order. Any success would be popular with the majority of tenants and the damaging weakness in demand for huge tracts of social housing might be overcome.

Social landlords have common law responsibilities relating to their tenants' right to peaceful enjoyment of their homes. It would be absurd to argue that they should never evict people for bad behaviour or have rules which they enforce. The danger lies in making these instruments the main pillar of order in and around housing estates and in substituting sanctions which may rest on allegation and hearsay for criminal procedures in cases where the latter would be appropriate. The faults of the adversarial approach are adopted without the compensating evidence-based criminal procedures. The alternative of mediation seems to be too often ignored, especially where neighbours are pitted against each other. The preventive role which other services could play is barely developed.

A theme running through this study is the association of tough enforcement with areas of low demand for social housing, which of course reflects wider structural change. The enforcement policy has achieved some local successes but it can, of course, do nothing to restore the jobs, improve the schools, provide the youth services or support the families whose troublesome children have given rise to much of the targeted behaviour. These things lie outside landlords' remit and there is not much they can do if others are not meeting these needs. Even so, some are trying, and there are several examples of estate-based social initiatives, such as projects aimed at improving children's attitudes and behaviour, which have been introduced and run by housing managers. In these efforts often the most stalwart partners of the housing departments have been—not social services, not education, but the police. The growing tendency for housing management and local police to make common cause is understandable, given that the aim is to reduce crime and disorder in social housing. But, like much else in this scenario, it gives pause for thought and calls for a look at the wider implications of these recent developments.

Discussion can be conducted at two levels: (a) effectiveness, and (b) social justice and political meanings or consequences. Effectiveness has to include reconciling a rule-based management style with the main aim of social housing which is to provide homes for people in need. More directly, it must be shown that civil law procedures are indeed an appropriate way of maintaining order and reducing crime on housing estates. As to the possible socio-political outcomes, any discussion has to acknowledge the right to a decent level of order for even (or especially) the poorest people; has to address notions of 'exclusion', 'exclusivity' and the management of diversity; and has to raise issues connected with information sharing and the potential stigmatising of individuals and groups within society. Both parts of this discussion have to include the context of the new powers and responsibilities placed at local level in the Crime and Disorder Act 1998.

RULES AND NORMS

For rules and rule-enforcement to work, the first condition is that people should understand what the rules are and that they apply to them. Social landlords are scrapping obscurely worded, small-print documents for plain language and user-friendly layout;[1] more importantly, there is growing emphasis on a meeting at the signing stage which drives home the many obligations involved, including those concerning the behaviour of everybody in the house. One authority (Sunderland) even has a policeman present at this point just to emphasise what it is about. Can this have any connection with the reported fears of the Sunderland parents (p.114, n)? Some of them had children in local authority care in connection with criminal charges, and were unwilling to have them back home for fear of eviction.

Clearly the agreement and its presentation is intended as an educative process, albeit one which does not hide the big stick. As with any such process, the people who need it most are likely to be least affected. Much more follow-up and on-going support and monitoring might be required to keep these households from being a nuisance to their neighbours, perhaps along the lines of the Dundee project (pp.69-70). Subjecting everybody to the same legal constraint looks undiscriminatory and has a certain declaratory force; it provides management with a stick to wave as a means to securing compliance, but cannot guarantee that behavioural norms will prevail evenly throughout the neighbourhood.

Given that housing need, rather than apple-pie standards, is supposed to be the criterion for granting a tenancy in the social sector, there will always be people pushing at the limits of accepted behaviour. Where the line is drawn depends much on the attitudes of other people in the neighbourhood. Perhaps the best argument for clear-cut written rules is that they strengthen the hand not so much of the landlord as of other tenants. This is a good reason for keeping a few basic obligations, especially the traditional ones like not playing loud music or leaving

---

[1] Oldham council won a Plain English Society award for its no-holds barred tenancy agreement. This document has an innocent-looking child's drawing on the cover although closer inspection suggests that the little pink-faced girl with plaits is hitting the little brown-faced girl over the head with a fire-cracker — it is doubtful whether this is the intended message.

rubbish on the stairs. Certain people might have to make individual undertakings—not necessarily formal contracts—such as drug misusers being made to understand that they must not cause nuisance in the neighbourhoods where they have been housed.[2] There can be no justification for the attempt to control mildly anti-social conduct by tenants that occurs outside their immediate neighbourhood, such as being drunk in public in a street in another part of town. Piling on tenancy conditions of this kind is little more than window dressing, given that repossession on such grounds would have to be shown to be reasonable.

Overemphasis on the tenancy agreement as a way of changing behaviour has other disadvantages, as pointed out by Karn *et al* (p. 15).[3] They believe that:

excessive reliance on enforcing tenancy agreements as the sole strategy for neighbour disputes unrealistically assumes that "guilt" can be established and it gives aggrieved tenants an exaggerated view of the powers of the local authority or housing association to enforce tenancy agreements. *A tenant is implicitly encouraged to demand that their neighbour is evicted or otherwise disciplined.* [italics added]

Unfortunately subsequent legislation, in the Housing Act 1996, took local authority practice further down this road. There is no provision in law or in tenancy agreements for action short of repossession; naturally social landlords are reluctant to proceed this far in most cases so they can only fall back on verbal warnings and warning letters, which if they fail can only be followed by notices of seeking possession. The alternative approach of mediation for neighbour disputes is surprisingly little used by local authority enforcers, whether from social landlords or environmental health departments (respectively 15.1 per cent and 1.4 per cent in Dignan's survey, pp.18-19).[4] There is no obligation to attempt mediation before seeking an anti-social behaviour order and the method gets only brief mention in government guidelines as one of several things which might be tried first.

Neighbour disputes involving lesser forms of harassment or crime have been successfully dealt with by mediation, although this may be after the possibility of prosecution has been rejected. Only 4.5 per cent of cases brought to housing managers involve more serious harassment or criminal activity (Dignan, p.89) and here prosecution must presumably be more likely to be pursued. It might seem strange that the rise in

---

[2] Advisory Council on the Misuse of Drugs, *Drug Misuse and the Environment* (London, Home Office, 1998) par. 7.5.

[3] op.cit.

[4] Dignan *et al*, op.cit.

reliance by social landlords on civil injunctions as a means of keeping individuals away from defined areas has taken place in response to serious crimes which by any definition should be the responsibility of the police and the courts. In fact, as we have seen (*Chapter 4*) these methods were adopted either in support of police operations or when the criminal process was judged to have failed. The main reason for the desire to target individuals was on account of intimidation of witnesses and general terrorising of areas by individuals or groups—all potentially criminal matters. The preference for civil actions was because the lower standard of proof made it possible to obtain a court order without being dependent on the appearance of intimidated witnesses.

Witness protection is fundamental

But, as the collapse of the Finnie case (pp.104-105) showed, this may be only a temporary reprieve. If an injunction is appealed, witnesses will nearly always have to appear in person for proof 'beyond reasonable doubt'. Exactly the same will apply to the anti-social behaviour order, so it is not easy to see what advantage this new injunction-type order will bring where it is firmly opposed by somebody not shy of intimidating witnesses—or where it is appealed and potential witnesses fear retaliation even though no threats have been uttered.

The issue which has done so much to muddy distinctions between civil and criminal matters is quite clearly witness intimidation. Measures providing further protection for vulnerable criminal witnesses at court have been incorporated in the Youth Justice and Criminal Evidence Act 1999 as recommended in the June 1998 report, *Speaking Up For Justice.*[5] The report was mainly concerned with pre-trial considerations and court procedures but also recommended a number of police practices to reduce intimidation at ground level so as to encourage reporting and improve investigation. It recommended that witness protection measures should be adopted within crime and disorder partnerships, and this is now official policy. Criminal proceedings should be taken against intimidators (where identifiable) as a matter of priority, for example under section 51 Criminal Justice and Public Order Act 1994,[6] although it is also suggested that 'where appropriate' anti-social behaviour orders, Housing Act 1996 powers or the Protection from Harassment Act 1997 could be applied. It is not clear why, with the wide powers against

---

[5] Home Office, op.cit.

[6] Section 51 of the 1994 Act created two offences: (a) intimidating a witness in the course of a criminal investigation; and (b) harming or threatening to harm a witness after the trial. Witness intimidation is also covered by the common law offence of perverting the course of justice.

intimidation in the 1994 and 1997 Acts, the report's authors thought that ASBOs and tenancy procedures might also be needed.

Local government representatives on the witness protection working group were keen to stress that civil witnesses, in Housing Act cases for example, are likewise sometimes at risk of intimidation. Although not within its remit, the report nevertheless made some recommendations on their behalf, notably that section 51 Criminal Justice and Public Order Act should be extended to civil cases—a move which might provide more long-term witness protection than relying on injunctions. It also proposed that the various administrative measures which it recommended to protect witnesses should be available in civil court cases, including the use of physical devices in the courtroom to protect anonymity. (Given the few civil cases likely to need this degree of protection, it has been suggested that these might be transferred to suitably equipped criminal courtrooms). A Government response to these proposals was at the time of writing still awaited.

Meanwhile the Social Exclusion Unit had a remit to report by December 1999 on any further action needed with regard to anti-social behaviour over and above the Crime and Disorder Act provisions. This looks rather like putting the cart before the horse. If more witness protection and firmer pursuit of intimidators had been an earlier priority (and even without extra powers this has sometimes been proved possible)[7] the arguments which supported the introduction of the anti-social behaviour order would have evaporated. However, the involvement of the Social Exclusion Unit is to be welcomed, given the urgent need to take a holistic approach to nuisance behaviour.

A class of housing outcasts?

Evictions and injunctions can be shown to have brought relief to areas plagued by small groups of persistent and violent offenders because the associates or family involved are then dispersed and lose their power. Unless the conditions which allow such people to impose themselves also change, the relief may again only be temporary. But sometimes, as is reported to have happened on the often-quoted Kingsmead Estate, Hackney, getting rid of a few high-profile offenders opens the way for new community projects which help to build confidence and strengthen social controls.

The expulsionary force of injunctions and/or Housing Act powers can therefore at times provide a degree of crime restraint in particular areas. It may well end up displacing criminal activity elsewhere, or even seeding it more widely. Little enough is known about what happens to people who are forced out of estates by these means. Such is the current

---

7 S Morris, op.cit.

turnover in many parts of the country between the social housing sector and the lower end of the private sector that when complaints are heard about the activities of new arrivals in a street there is no knowing whether they have been ejected from social housing or have left of their own accord. Systems for tracking what happens to people banished from social housing need to be adopted, as recommended by NACRO in its survey of local authority practice.[8]

Most seriously, repossession based on bad conduct risks making some of the more vulnerable people homeless, or at any rate without access to social housing. The growing practice of removing somebody's right to be even considered for a tenancy on grounds of what officials know, or think they know, about them is a still more serious engine of exclusion because it affects so many more people (*Chapter 5*). The housing director of NACRO has warned of the creation of 'a new class of the unhouseable', which risks 'undermining the underlying goal for a more inclusive and safer society'.[9] Everything that has been said in the present study should underline the importance of that warning. *Of all the issues raised in this book, this is the most important*, because, as the practice of information sharing grows, ever more areas and sectors of the rented market will be barred to people with reputations as 'nuisance neighbours'.

To recapitulate, the various ways in which people may be so barred are:

- by having been evicted for bad behaviour from social housing,

- by leaving a social tenancy voluntarily but with a reputation as a troublemaker,

- by applying to join the housing register and being obliged to declare past, convictions or by having such convictions revealed by police to the local authority,

- by being 'blacklisted' by one social landlord who has passed the information on to the authority which maintains the register in the area, who may then inform other social landlords,

- by being disqualified from the register for reasons of conduct and this information then having been conveyed to private landlords,

---

8 Warburton *et al*, op.cit.
9 Tim Bell, 'Housing Exclusion', Safer Society, No. 1, October 1998, 21-22.

- by applying to join a particular housing scheme but finding that rules drawn up at the request of tenants exclude people with certain convictions or records of misbehaviour,

- not being formally disqualified from rehousing, but just not being offered a tenancy.

That is not to say that housing managers should have no policy towards tenants who behave badly—far from it. In the past, after all, such people may have been equally troublesome, but by various, not always commendable, devices they were contained. Today, someone who has seriously upset the neighbours through persistent nuisance may well have to be moved elsewhere by the landlord, but could be offered a tenancy with extra supervision or support. Repossession following a criminal conviction imposes a double jeopardy which should be avoided as much as possible. It could be limited to a small category of offences such as serious racial harassment or serious intimidatory violence which suggest that the rights of other tenants will continue to be significantly infringed if the offender remains in the social housing sector. Even then, following up the banished households and providing whatever support package they will accept is desirable in the interests of their private sector neighbours as well as themselves.

Enforcement is not the same as protection
Legal powers based on property rights and the administrative powers that go with them do not seem very effective at ensuring protection for people who are the victims of violence and harassment by social tenants. If they move out because they cannot bear it any longer they may be deemed intentionally homeless. If they are owner occupiers being victimised by social tenants they can only try to persuade the landlord to take enforcement action. The courts have been reluctant to accept landlords' liability in such cases.[10] The case of *Smith v Scott*[11] held that that Lewisham Council was not liable for the nuisance caused to neighbours by their tenants and the principle was upheld in the *Hussain* case (p.68). This resulted in a judgement that Lancaster City Council had no 'duty of care' towards the victims despite the appalling level and persistence of harassment being suffered. It was argued by the plaintiffs that the council had taken no effective action against the perpetrators despite numerous undertakings to do so. Warnings from housing managers had done nothing to abate the trouble nor had an injunction brought under the Highways Act against one perpetrator who was not a

---

[10] Hunter and Bretherton, op.cit., 23 et seq.
[11] *Smith v. Scott and Others* [1973] Ch 314

tenant. For years no effective prosecutions were mounted by the police until evidence was provided by a television crew (indeed the plaintiff himself was prosecuted when he tried to defend himself).

Racial harassment of the degree suffered in this case certainly belongs in the criminal courts, and the limitations of landlord and tenant law to protect third party victims should underline the need for effective prosecution and prompt police intervention. The combination of the post-Lawrence inquiry prerogatives and the sections of the Crime and Disorder Act 1998 relating to racially aggravated crime should prevent similar extreme cases in future. The new local strategies for crime and disorder will also hopefully focus action on the more low level racial harassment which is endemic in many neighbourhoods.

The whole field of tenancy enforcement becomes daily more complex as further areas of former council owned and managed property are tranferred to other types of social tenancy, officially known as Registered Social Landlords (RSLs). The existing RSLs (especially the established housing asociations who used to be able to control their own intake) complain of worsening experience of anti-social behaviour and are demanding parity of powers with local government to deal with it.[12] Within many council run estates, there are blocks of RSL property as well as varied proportions of owner-occupied dwellings; all of which makes a tenure-based system of behaviour control increasingly questionable. Owner-occupiers who are a serious nuisance to tenant neighbours pose a particular problem, especially in Scotland where there is no general local authority power to bring interdicts and Scottish authorities may see the anti-social behaviour order as their opportunity. Meanwhile, enforcement-minded local authority landlords are trying to train other social landlords in their way of thinking. Current policies, which are hastening the de-municipalisation of social housing at the same time as providing councils with more powers against disorder, indicate that in future elected councils will have less to do with hands-on housing management and more to do with overseeing the policing of poor tenants.

Making parents make their children behave

The difficulty of reconciling two different aims—that of providing homes for people who need them most and that of keeping social housing free of crime and disorder—is most evident when one considers the disproportionate number of poor families with children who end up in the less attractive social housing schemes. More children usually means

---

[12] *Nuisance News*, No. 8, December 1998.

more mess and damage,[13] producing conditions which make the area more unattractive. Anne Power has remarked,[14] in connection with her study of hard-to-let estates, that '[nothing] could represent more vividly the failure of public housing than the use of numbers of children as an actual measure of unpopularity'. The attitudes and tensions between children and youths on the one hand, and older residents on the other, have been discussed earlier (*Chapter 3*). The presence of a high proportion of children with behavioural difficulties,[15] combined with conditions favourable to youth offending, means that the 'anti-social' label is most likely to attach to the young. Punishment by eviction is a particularly inappropriate response, especially when the parents have done all they can, and repossession orders sometimes fail for this reason. Invoking parental responsibility and punishing parents for the misdeeds of their children is an increasingly prominent part of the criminal justice system[16] and housing law and practice encourage the same response.[17]

It is fair to say that, in the great majority of cases, invoking parental responsibility in the context of tenancy enforcement goes no further than informal warnings, and if handled reasonably can be a positive force for better behaviour. Parents and children may be asked to attend for interview at the neighbourhood office and a non-confrontational discussion is usually enough to secure improved behaviour—with, of course, the understanding that any further complaints will trigger a notice about seeking possession.

These tactics seem to have been used to some effect in Salford, where as many as 20 families were warned in this manner after groups of youths from an estate were said to have been causing damage and intimidation 'in the locality' of the estate, including a local shopping centre.[18] Yet even this apparently well-handled case raises wider issues. Almost all the youths denied the accusations against them—and they

---

[13] A 1978 Home Office Research report found that more than six children aged six to 16 per ten dwellings caused vandalism to increase significantly. Sheena Wilson, 'Vandalism "Defensible Space" on London Housing Estates', in *Tackling Vandalism*, R V G Clarke, ed., HORS 47 (London, Home Office, 1978).

[14] Power (1989), op.cit.

[15] In the poorest families, 20 per cent of boys and 15 per cent of girls aged four to 15 are said to have emotional/behavioural difficulties. *The Health of Young People 1995-97* (London, Department of Health).

[16] Loraine Gelsthorpe, op.cit.

[17] In *Manchester City Council v. Hutton* (17 February 1999), Housing Act 1996 injunctions (prohibiting anti-social behaviour) were sought against tenants largely relying on allegations of repeated nuisance by the children of the family. The judge dismissed the application, saying that section 152 did not cover actions by others. Reported in *Legal Action*, April 1999.

[18] *Nuisance News*, No. 3, September 1997.

were only accusations, supplied by police and 'some community leaders'. There was hostility between police and youths in the area and in this context the involvement of the housing authority in curbing disorderly behaviour outside the estate itself looks rather too close to what would normally be regarded as the job of the police, but with a potential sanction—loss of family home—far in excess of normal punishments for public disorder. The account of the process admits anxiety on the part of housing officers that in taking this role they will attract to themselves the hostility expressed towards the police. And they acknowledge that long-term solutions lie outside their sphere, but need to be addressed by provision of better facilities for under 25s and tackling the issue of school exclusions.

Judges have sometimes expressed concern at the doubtful justice of evicting parents who are simply unable to control their difficult children. In the case of *Darlington Borough Council v Sterling* (1997)[19] the district judge clearly felt sympathy for Mrs Sterling, whose 13-year old son was creating havoc in the neighbourhood with fires, stone-throwing, knife-wielding, assaults and other aggression. He said that '[it] was not fair to lay the fault for her son's behaviour on her. He was difficult to control' He believed that as a result she should not be held to be intentionally homeless, and he hoped that the council would find her somewhere else to live, staying a possession order for three months to allow this to happen. The order was overturned in the county court but reinstated on appeal. The judgement emphasised that the district judge had no power to order the council to rehouse anybody but that in the circumstances he was correct to put the rights of the neighbours above those of the Sterlings.

In a similar (unreported) case in the Midlands the judge made the point that a child who was beyond parental control would be better dealt with under the Children Act 1989 rather than being seen as the trigger for a possession order. This would seem the obviously right approach, yet in this case social services had already declined to act. What appears to be an area of concern crying out for co-ordination between housing authorities, social services and education too often demonstrates how far local authorities have to go to work effectively across departments where families are concerned.[20] Some of the most problematic kinds of behaviour—such as racial harassment which often involves youthful

---

[19] 29 HLR 309.

[20] Interestingly, this very point was made in a commentary on a similar case in Gosport by the co-ordinator of the Social Landlords' Crime and Nuisance Group, Tim Winter. But Gosport's Housing Manager, Charles Harman, was unrepentant, stating that 'if eviction is the most effective and available solution it needs to be used'. *Nuisance News*, No. 7, September 1998.

perpetrators—need to be approached not merely by punishment but by education, mediation and local strategies to break down prejudice.

In the vacuum created by non-co-ordination of effort, it is both predictable and depressing that in local authority circles the anti-social behaviour order (section 1 Crime and Disorder Act 1998) has been warmly welcomed for the extra strength that it provides for proceedings taken against ten to 17 year-olds (See *Chapter 5*). Quite specifically this is viewed, especially by housing departments, as providing new weaponry against the age-group which causes them most trouble. In a number of authorities housing departments are taking the lead on community safety, or if not in charge, have managed to retain control over the ASBO. Government guidance[21] on the use of ASBOs has veered towards favouring their use for 12 to 17 year olds, only advising restraint in their use for ten and eleven-year-olds. Given the political rhetoric surrounding the creation of the order this should have come as no surprise.

The Blair government may even be hoping to brandish statistics on ASBOs and child curfews imposed as part of their re-election strategy. Otherwise, why the impatience of the Prime Minister and Home Secretary, in statements early in September 1999?[22] Deploring the lack so far of any curfew orders and the imposition of barely any anti-social behaviour orders[23] the Home Secretary issued a 'sharp reminder' to councils to get their act together. This produced an equally sharp response from local government representatives, pointing out that the 1998 Act was designed to produce local, not central, decision-making, and that procedures set by government involved extensive consultation.

ASBOs are anyway seen by most councils as intended only for exceptional cases (and as this book has emphasised, they have many alternative choices of action). Child curfews for under tens (apparently, and inconsequentially, linked by the Prime Minister in his *Observer* interview to his moral crusade against teenage pregnancies) are likely to be even more exceptional. The non-utility of section 14 Crime and Disorder Act 1998 could well prove a source of long-term embarrassment to the Government.

---

[21] Home Office (1999), op.cit.

[22] *Observer*, 5 May 1999 and *Guardian*, 7 September 1999.

[23] North Somerset imposed an ASBO on a man who had been harassing council housing staff; Liverpool imposed ASBOs on two teenagers, banning them from certain streets. In Scotland—outside Mr Straw's jurisdiction—a woman in Dundee was an early ASBO recipient.

THE FUTURE OF LOCAL ORDER

These early signs suggest that it is quite likely that the cost and complexity of imposing anti-social behaviour orders will mean that they will not assume great prominence within the huge panoply of behaviour control which already exists, and the further range of disciplines for children and parents provided in the Crime and Disorder Act 1998. Much will depend on what sort of culture will drive the local crime and disorder strategies demanded by the 1998 Act and what priorities and practices emerge. These are important questions which by definition will find different answers in different local areas. Districts which already have strong commitments to 'tough' policies—be it 'zero-tolerance' policing, curfews, or tenancy enforcement—may continue to be driven by these. But the obligation to work in partnership across different agencies—and this will only succeed if it includes inter-departmental co-operation within local authorities—should help to raise awareness of the wider implications of simplistic law and order approaches. The intial crime audits were conducted against unrealistic deadlines but at least some will have already thrown up fresh considerations about what constitutes crime and disorder and who is affected.

The 'partnership' style of working has already been widely practised in the crime prevention context for specific projects, but the scale and strategic remit of the new system is something quite different. Partnerships have been defined by Crawford[24] as of broadly two kinds: 'multi-agency', which may be little more than forming a committee involving all interested agencies without any significant change in the way they operate; and 'inter-agency', where working practices are adapted to fit in with each other and new structures may be formed. The second model is the one which is meant to prevail in the crime and disorder partnerships. It cannot be expected to win through everywhere, given the power relationships and internal politics involved. A pattern which is repeated in many local 'partnership' schemes is that one or two dominant partners run the process and others are sidelined:[25] something that the government says it wants to avoid and the foreword to the bulky guidance document[26] seeks to erase the impression that police and local authorities are all that count.

---

[24] Crawford, A, op.cit., 118-123.

[25] Pearson *et al*, op.cit.; Gelsthorpe and Liddle, op.cit.

[26] *Crime and Disorder Act 1998: Guidance on Statutory Crime and Disorder Partnerships* (London, Home Office, 1998).

The other theme running through the system is that of 'community'. The local community must be consulted on crime and disorder priorities and this is intended to be an integral part of the policy-making process. It must be right to provide means for the citizenry to have a part in decisions which touch their concerns so directly. But the over-used and under-defined concept of community is a slippery foundation. Often it provides a convenient means to recruit compliance with centrally driven purposes, and this is especially true in the context of crime control. Moreover it ignores diversity by implying shared opinions and values among the citizens of a given area or within artificially constructed sub-groups such as 'the black community' or 'the gay community'. At worst it encourages exclusivity and a shutting-out of people who do not 'belong'. As Crawford has warned,[27] '[appeals] to community, overlaid upon today's social and economic realities, may serve to entrench, extend, and legitimise inequalities. They can all too easily conceal questions about the relative distribution of social and economic disadvantage, including safety from crime.'

The struggle to lay claim to a share of public order and safety is nowhere more obvious than in the increasingly unstable and fragmented social housing sector and associated parts of the private housing market. While those at the top of the urban housing ladder can buy into 'safe' areas and physical defences, those at the very bottom, in the poorest private ownership and rentals and the most unpopular council estates, have fewest defences and most exposure to crime. In between, at various stages of the housing ladder, people are endeavouring to preserve or improve their own tranquillity and the market values that go with them. They feel threatened when (as happened in the early 1990s and could happen again any time there is an economic downturn) having bought a property on a new private development, the market deteriorates and they find that their neighbours have become tenants installed by a social landlord (a situation which has led to petitions and protests). Private housing estates built within or alongside problem council estates as part of the process of regeneration may be especially vulnerable. Residents of one such development of relatively expensive houses on Merseyside refused to remove the high fence installed as temporary building-site protection which divided them from a poor council estate and also succeeded in blocking off the road which ran beside it.[28]

---

[27] Crawford, A, op.cit. (1997), 275. This paragraph owes much to his analysis of the uses of community in local crime prevention.

[28] This is not, of course, a new phenomenon. For example a long running battle in Oxford began in the 1930s over a physical barrier erected between an area of private housing and a council estate. But at least the matter was seen as

This becomes a process which in various forms repeats itself inside social housing too. People who might be regarded as unwelcome neighbours by well-off house-owners often have even more reason to try and cocoon themselves from still-less welcome neighbours. At the end of the line, communities (sic) which are now recognised by the government as 'socially excluded' regard the removal and exclusion of some of their number as a prerequisite to gaining a modicum of those precious commodities, safety and order. Some of those removed may go on to become a real or perceived threat to order in new neighbourhoods, thereby raising the temperature of fear and suspicion.

The near-hysteria generated in local areas by the subject of housing convicted paedophiles has led to horrible attacks on quite innocent men, sometimes led by people who seem to find this an outlet for violence. The child-molester has become the pre-eminent sinister stranger and hostililty rides high in poor estates where people are no doubt conscious of being less protected than the inhabitants of better-off neighbourhoods. Individual high-risk offenders are rightly a cause of great concern to all agencies involved in rehousing. But there is growing recognition that blanket bans will not work. Policies which seek to ring-fence council-owned housing by banning all known sex offenders can never succeed in their purpose, but they are formed in response to the instinct which sees the threat of crime as something to be resolved by keeping criminals out or kicking them out—whether by walls or by rules.

We are in a period of rapid change in social housing, as a process begun under the Conservative government continues to create much more diversity in ownership and management, in most cases designed to provide far more input by tenants in running the property. New tenants will still only come from the housing register, and may not always be acceptable to tenants' groups. Structures are not generally supposed to permit tenants to veto new arrivals; indeed some of the best management schemes try by means of 'welcoming committees' and the like to establish good relations with newcomers, also seen as an aid to good behaviour. But where tenants are permitted to lay down rules of entry—as in many co-operative schemes for example—they may be more stringent than the former council rules. The results are often impressive—better kept property and less disorder—and a greater sense of trust between neighbours. Tenant power has been preached[29] as the secret of improved neighbourhoods, has been shown to work and cannot be begrudged. All that needs to be done at this stage is to sound a note of

controversial. Peter Collinson, *The Cotteslowe Walls: A Study in Social Class* (London, Faber and Faber, 1963).

[29] Especially in the writings of Anne Power, following many years studying estate improvement schemes.

voice will be heard: the well organized tenant group or the bed-sit families still waiting for a tenancy?

When faced with unlettable estates, some councils are encouraging tenants to form their own enclaves with other people that they feel safe with, which in some places means people who can show that they have no record for certain crimes (p.130). It is hoped that by this method stability can be regained. For the same reason different generations of the same family may now be given preferential choice to move into the same neighbourhood, in places where there is little other reason for anyone to want to settle. This can be the best form of neighbourhood support and solidarity. In other words the prioritising of need in every housing allocation is no longer seen as the way to ensure stability and order, or to keep properties occupied. But then what happens to the needy? New legislation has been promised, in order to relax the rules on 'need' as top priority in the interests of promoting 'mixed communities',[30] a term which actually means letting houses to smaller proportions of poor, unemployed people.

What kind of order, then, awaits the people of those neighbourhoods today marked by the blight of deprivation and exclusion? Will it depend on regulation, enforcement and banishment of the bad? Will it rely on increased separation of the 'respectable' and the 'dangerous', with the latter subject to ever-greater degrees of policing and surveillance? Or will the reliance on formal regulation, on anti-social behaviour orders and child curfews, on the definition of communities in terms of crime prevention, be steadily diminished as access is provided to a better share in opportunities and the means of using them? The change from exclusion to inclusion in mainstream society is now recognised as a many faceted process, of which control of crime and disorder is only a part. People vary in the extent to which they prioritise this aspect and which bits they mind about most. If only certain voices are listened to a distorted form of normality with a fragile basis risks being enforced.

Achieving more stable neighbourhoods is a legitimate and critical policy aim, but short-cut methods which define communities solely in terms of crime prevention and the absence of bad behaviour rely on the sterile concepts of disease-elimination. To quote Crawford[31] again: 'crime may be an inappropriate vehicle around which to construct open and tolerant communities. Those who champion community safety and communtarianism may be injecting, albeit unwittingly, a pernicious new

---

[30] *Inside Housing*, 5 February 1999.

[31] Adam Crawford, 'Community Safety and the Quest for Security: Holding Back the Dynamics of Social Exclusion', Policy Studies, 19.3/4 (December 1998) 237-253.

dynamic into strained social relations as the boundaries of "community" are increasingly constructed around "defensive exclusivity"'.

Several years ago Colin Sumner identified a new mind-set, which he called 'the sociology of censure'. This ideology he believes has replaced the more individualist notions of 'delinquency' and 'deviance'. It relies on imposing from above order through regulations which are justified by appeals to general moral principles:

> The concept of social censure registers several key features of modern practices of social regulation: their political character, their reliance on value judgements, and their formal, bureaucratic character.[32]

The *politicisation* of housing bureaucracies within the 'law and order' climate of the 1990s is precisely the problem faced by those who would aim for a more inclusive and less rule-dominated approach. There are people in positions of responsibility within social housing who are well aware of the danger of being driven in the wrong direction. The Chief Executive of the Worcester Housing Association[33] fears that the good intentions of the Social Exclusion Unit will be swamped by the imperatives of the Crime and Disorder Act and the media hype on nuisance neighbours, and he is not alone. There is implicit tension at local level between those (often elected councillors) who press for tougher action against individuals and others who well understand that formal exclusion is not the end of the problem.

There are many people working in local government who agree that real solutions must address causation and offer troublesome people a way out of their behaviour patterns. Small steps are being taken in small scale settings: social services providing community support for alcoholic tenants; schools engaging children in projects which foster a sense of 'ownership' of their local surroundings; youth workers or even housing officers thinking up ways in which the gulf between young and old can be bridged. Breaking down stereotypes, reducing fear or a sense of worthlessness, valuing people and places for their own sake: any one of these results helps to combat the labels which express dislike, disapproval and the typology of social censure.

Anticipating the needs of vulnerable tenants can pay big dividends in terms of reduction of nuisance and disorder. Provision of rehousing support to mentally disordered tenants, especially to former in-patients, is one obvious requirement. A far bigger one is that of very young people, especially those separated from their families for one reason or another, who are increasingly appearing among new social tenants.

---

32 Colin Sumner, op.cit., 35.

33 Article by Peter Brown, *The Guardian*, 15 April 1998.

More landlords could copy Derby City Council, which now has a Young Persons' Housing Officer, dedicated to helping the transition to independent living and making youthful tenants understand why they need to be considerate to neighbours when it comes to noise, rubbish etc. This makes it less likely that these younger residents will become automatically branded as 'nuisances'.[34]

It is hardly original to say that inclusive methods involve working across service boundaries and identifying problems at an early stage. The statutory crime and disorder strategies do offer an opportunity. No doubt, also, this is what the the Social Exclusion Unit will be preaching in its consideration of anti-social behaviour and indeed all the categories of neighbourhood problem that it has decided to address. Many of those working in the field reached the same conclusion long ago, but still face great obstacles in making anything happen. Issues relating to children, youths, the mentally ill and the racially harassed all call for an integrated approach; and integration must include not only the service providers but the tenants themselves. Ordinary people are not necessarily as intolerant as the louder voices among them sometimes make them appear. Good housing managers can contribute to this. This is not the place to try and tell them how, but a story from Scotland will serve to make the point.

A drug-ridden and vandalised estate in Glasgow began to improve with the help of a strong tenants' committee and a plain-speaking housing manager. New tenants with convictions for drug dealing or housebreaking had to show that they were rehabilitated. A woman who had been a former resident with a record of prostitution and drug dealing wanted to come back to the estate. She had been on probation with a drug treatment programme. She was interviewed by the housing manager with tenants' representatives on the letting committee. These were volunteers who had received training in their role but were not allowed a veto. Her drug counsellor was with her and, though saying nothing, his presence vouched for her veracity when she declared that she had overcome her habit and was looking for work. The tenants welcomed her back and one of them offered to introduce her to a potential employer.

A simplistic approach which sees the exclusion of criminal troublemakers as essential to the 'rescue' of marginalised estates[35] does not provide a permanent answer. Not only will excluded households frequently reappear in similar circumstances, but their future as non-trouble-makers would be much better secured by re-integrative processes such as described in the above case. The potential of 'tenant-

---

[34] *Nuisance News*, September 1999.
[35] see the recommendations of Anne Power, op.cit. (1997).

power' as a form of social glue has much to recommend it provided it is structured in ways which prioritise restorative rather than divisive methods. Managerial styles which rely on rule enforcement rather than shared solutions are short-term, stigmatising and encourage tenants to demand ever-tougher responses to unpopular behaviour. This is likely to continue until resources, shared casework, community mediation and other strands come together to strengthen the boundaries of reasonable behaviour and provide a way back for those who exceed them.

Bibliography

Abbreviations

CDA: *Crime and Disorder Act 1998*
EPA: *Environmental Protection Act 1990*
ER/All ER: *All England Law Reports*
HOC/HC: *House of Commons*
HL: *House of Lords*
HMSO: *Her Majesty's Stationery Office*
EGLR: *Estates Gazette Law Reports*
HLR: *Housing Law Reports*
NACRO: *National Association for the Care and Resettlement of Offenders*
PRO: *Public Records Office*
WLR: *Weekly Law Reports*

Advisory Council on the Misuse of Drugs, *Drug Misuse and the Environment* (London, Home Office, 1998).

Alexander, G. S., 'Civic Property', *Social and Legal Studies*, 6.2 (1997), 217-234.

Ashworth, Andrew, Gardner, John, Morgan, Rod, Smith, A. T. H., von Hirsch, Andrew and Wasik, Martin, 'Neighbouring on the Oppressive: the Government's Community Safety Order" Proposals', *Criminal Justice*, 16:1, (1998) 7-14.

Association of Metropolitan Authorities, *Crime Reduction. A Framework for the Nineties?* (London, AMA, 1990).

Baldwin, John, ' Problem Housing Estates—Perceptions of Tenants, City Officials and Criminologists', *Social and Economic Administration*, Vol. 8, (1974), 116-135.

Baldwin, John and Bottoms, Anthony, *The Urban Criminal* (London, Tavistock, 1976).

Barke, Michael and Turnbull, Guy, *Meadowell: The Biography of an 'Estate with Problems'* (Aldershot, Avebury, 1992).

Baumgartner, M. P., 'Social Control in Suburbia', in D. Black (ed), *Towards a General Theory of Social Control* (Orlando, Flo., Academic Press, 1984).

Bell, Tim, 'Housing Exclusion', *Safer Society*, No.1, October 1998.

Blakely, E. J. and Snyder, M. G., *Fortress America. Gated Communities in the United States.* (Washington D.C., Brookings Institution Press, 1997).

Bottoms, Anthony, 'Environmental Criminology', in M. Maguire, R. Morgan, and R. Reiner (eds), *The Oxford Handbook of Criminology,* 2nd edition (Oxford, Oxford University Press, 1997).

Bottoms, Anthony, Mawby, Rob and Xanthos, Polii, 'A Tale of Two Estates' in D. Downes (ed), *Crime and the City. Essays in Memory of John Barron Mays* (Basingstoke, Macmillan, 1989).

Bottoms, Anthony and Wiles, Paul, 'Housing tenure and residential crime careers in Britain' in A. Reiss and M. Tonry (eds), *Communities and Crime. Crime and Justice: a review of research .* Vol. 8 (Chicago, University of Chicago Press, 1986).

— 'Housing Markets and Residential Crime Careers. A case study from Sheffield' in D. Evans, N. Fyfe and D. Herbert, (eds), *Crime, Policing and Place* (London, Routledge, 1992).

— 'Crime and Insecurity in the City', in C. Fijnaut *et al* (eds), *Changes in Society, Crime and Criminal Justice. Volume 1. Crime and Insecurity in the City* (Antwerp, Kluwer Law International), 1995).

— 'Understanding Crime Prevention in Late Modern Societies', in Trevor Bennett (ed), *Preventing Crime and Disorder: Targeting Strategies and Responsibilities* (Cambridge, University of Cambridge Institute of Criminology, 1996).

Bowling, Benjamin, *Violent Racism* (Oxford, Clarendon Press, 1998).

Bright, Susan and Gilbert, Geoff, *Landlord and Tenant Law: the Nature of Tenancies* (Oxford, Clarendon Press, 1995).

Brown, Sheila, *Understanding Youth and Crime* (Buckingham, Open University Press, 1998).

Building Research Establishment, *Effects of Environmental Noise on People at Home.* BRE Information paper 22/93 (Construction Research Communications Ltd., 1993).

Burney, Elizabeth, *Housing on Trial* (London, Oxford University Press and Institute of Race Relations, 1967).

Burney, Elizabeth and Pearson, Geoffrey, 'Mentally Disordered Offenders: Finding the Focus for Diversion', *Howard Journal* 34:4 (November 1995), 291-311.

Burr, Angela, 'An inner-city Community Response to Heroin Use', in S. McGregor (ed), *Drugs and British Society* (London, Routledge, 1989).

Burrows, Roger and Rhodes, David, *Unpopular Places? Area Disadvantage and the Geography of Misery In England* (York, University of York, Centre for Housing Policy, 1998).

Bursik, Robert, 'Ecological Stability and the Dynamics of Delinquency' in A. Reiss and M. Tonry (eds) *Communities and Crime: Crime and Justice, a Review of Research* , Vol 8 (Chicago, Chicago University Press, 1986).

— 'Social Disorganisation and Theories of Crime and Delinquency: Problems and Prospects', *Criminology* 26, (1998), 519-551.

Butler, Sophie and Bacon, Nicola, Access Denied. *The Exclusion of People in Need From Social Housing* (London, Shelter, 1998).

Campbell, Beatrice, *Goliath: Britain's Dangerous Places* (London, Methuen, 1993).

Campbell, Sue, 'Gypsies: the Criminalisation of a Way of Life?', *Criminal Law Review* (1995), 28-37.

Central Housing Advisory Committee, *The Management of Municipal Housing Estates. First Report of the Housing Management Sub-Committee* (London, HMSO, 1938).

— *Unsatisfactory Tenants. Sixth Report of the Housing Management Sub-Committee* (London, HMSO, 1955).

— *Council Housing: Purposes, Priorities and Procedures, Ninth Report of the Housing Management Sub-Committee* ('The Cullingworth report') (London, HMSO, 1969).

Chartered Institute of Housing, (paper), *Rehousing Sex Offenders* (Coventry, CIH, February 1998).

Clapham, David, Kintrea, Keith, Malcolm, John, Parkey, Hilary and Scott, Suzie, *A Baseline Study of Housing Management in Scotland,* Centre for Housing Research and Urban Studies, University of Glasgow (Edinburgh, Scottish Office Central Research Unit, 1995).

Clapham, David, 'The Social Construction of Housing Management', *Urban Studies* 34 (1997),761-774.

Cohen, Stanley, 'Sociological Approaches to Vandalism', in Claude Levy-Leboyer (ed), *Vandalism: Behaviour and Motivations* (Amsterdam, Elsevier Science Publishers, 1984).

Coleman, Alice, *Utopia on Trial* (London, Hilary Shipman, 1985).

Collinson, Peter, *The Cottesloe Walls: A Study in Social Class* (London, Faber and Faber, 1963).

Corinna, L., *Housing Allocation Policy and Its Effects. A Case Study From Oldham CDP* (York, University of York, Department of Social Administration and Social Work, 1976).

Crawford, Adam, *The Local Governance of Crime: Appeals to Community and Partnerships* (Oxford, Clarendon Press, 1997).

— *Crime Prevention and Community Safety: Politics, Policies and Practice* (Harlow, Addison Wesley Longman, 1998).

—'Community Safety and the Quest for Security: Holding Back the Dynamics of Social Exclusion', *Policy Studies* 19:3/4 (1998), 237-253.

Cullingworth, J.B., *English Housing Trends, Occasional Papers on Social Administration*, Number 13 (London, G.Bell and Sons, 1965).

Damer, Sean, *From Moorepark to 'Wine Alley': the Rise and Fall of a Glasgow Housing Scheme* (Edinburgh, University of Edinburgh Press, 1989).

Department of Education and Employment, *More Willingly to School: An Independent Evaluation of the Truancy and Disaffected Pupils GEST Programme* (London, DEE, 1995).

Department of Environment, Housing Services Advisory Group Report, *Security on Council Estates* (London DoE, 1980)

— *Report of the Noise Review Working Party* ('The Batho report'), (London, HMSO, 1990).

— *Code of Guidance on Parts VI and VII of the Housing Act 1996. Allocation of Housing Accomodation: Homelessness* (London, DoE, December 1996).

— *Mapping Local Authority Estates Using the 1991 Index of Local Conditions* (London, DoE, 1997).

Department of Health, *The Health of Young People, 1995-97* (London, Stationery Office, 1998).

Dignan, James, Sorsby, Angela and Hibbert, James, *Neighbour Disputes: Comparing the Cost Effectiveness of Mediation and Alternative Approaches* (Sheffield, University of Sheffield Centre for Criminological and Legal Research, 1996).

Dorn, N., Murji, K. and South, N., *Traffickers: Drug Markets and Law Enforcement* (London, Routledge, 1992).

Evans, K., Fraser, P. and Walklate, S., 'Whom Can You Trust? The Politics of "Grassing" on an Inner City Housing Estate', *The Sociological Review*, 44:3 (1996), 361-380.

Farrall, Stephen, Bannister, Jon, Ditton, Jason and Gilchrist, Elizabeth, 'Questioning the Measurement of the "Fear of Crime": Findings from a Major Methodological Study', *British Journal of Criminology*, 37:4 (Autumn 1997), 658-679.

Farrell, Graham, 'Multiple Victimisation; Its Extent and Significance', *International Review of Victimology*, (1992), 85-102.

Farrington, David, 'Human Development and Criminal Careers', in M. Maguire, R. Morgan and R. Reiner (eds), *The Oxford Handbook of Criminology*, 2nd ed (Oxford, Clarendon Press, 1997).

Felson, Marcus, *Crime and Everyday Life* (London, Pine Forge Press, 1993).

Foster, Janet, 'Informal Social Control and Community Crime Prevention', *British Journal of Criminology*, 35:4 (Autumn 1995), 563-583.

Foster, Janet and Hope, Tim, *Housing, Community and Crime: the Impact of the Priority Estates Programme*, Home Office Research Study 131 (London, HMSO, 1993).

Garland, David, *Punishment and Welfare* (Aldershot, Gower, 1985).

Gelsthorpe, Loraine, 'Parents and Criminal Children', in A. Bainham, S. Day Sclater and M.Richards (eds), *What is a Parent?: A Socio-Legal Analysis* (Oxford, Hart Publishing, 1999).

Gelsthorpe, Loraine and Liddle, Mark, *Inter-agency Crime Prevention: Organising Local Delivery*, Crime Prevention Unit Paper 52 (London, Home Office, 1994).

Genn, Hazel, 'Multiple Victimisation' in M.Maguire and J. Pointing (eds), *Victims of Crime: A New Deal* (Milton Keynes, Open University Press, 1988).

Giddens, Anthony, *The Consequences of Modernity* (Cambridge, Polity Press, 1990).

Gill, Owen, *Luke Street: Housing Policy, Conflict and the Creation of a Delinquent Area* (London, Macmillan, 1977).

Graham, John and Bowling, Benjamin, *Young People and Crime*, Home Office Research Study 145, (London, Home Office, 1995).

Gray, Fred, 'Selection and Allocation in Council Housing', *Transactions of the British Institute of Geographers,* New Series 1 (1976), 34-45.

Gray, Kevin and Gray, Susan Francis, 'Civil Rights, Civil Wrongs and Quasi-public Space', *European Human Rights Law Review,* 1999, issue 1, 46-102.

Green Mazerolle, Lorraine and Roehl, Jan, (eds), *Civil Remedies and Crime Prevention,* Crime Prevention Studies Vol. 9 (Monsey, NY, Criminal Justice Press, 1998).Holmans, Alan, *Housing Policy in Britain* (Aldershot, Croom Helm, 1987).

Home Office, *Community Safety Order: A Consultation Paper* (London, Home Office, September 1997).

— *Speaking Up for Justice, Report of the Interdepartmental Working Group on the Treatment of Vulnerable or Intimidated Witnesses in the Criminal Justice System* (London, Home Office, 1998).

— *Crime and Disorder Act: Guidance on Statutory Crime and Disorder Partnerships* (London, Home Office, 1998)

— *Supporting Families: A Consultation Paper* (London, Home Office, 1998).

— *Crime and Disorder Act: Guidance on Anti-Social Behaviour Orders* (London, Home Office, 1999).

Hope, Tim, 'Communities, Crime and Inequality in England and Wales', in T. Bennett (ed), *Preventing Crime and Disorder: Targeting Strategies and Responsibilities* (Cambridge, University of Cambridge Institute of Criminology, 1996).

Hough, Michael, *Anxiety About Crime: Findings from the 1994 British Crime Survey,* Home Office research Study 147, (London, Home Office, 1995).

Housing Services Advisory Group, *Security on Council Estates* (London, Department of Environment, 1980).

Hunter, A., 'Private, Parochial and Public Order: The Problem of Crime and Incivility in Urban Communities', in G. D. Suttles and M.N. Zald, (eds), *The Challenge of Social Control* (Norwood, N. J., Ablex, 1985).

Hunter, Caroline, Mullen, Tom and Scott, Suzie, *Legal Remedies for Neighbour Nuisance: Comparing Scottish and English Approaches* (York, Joseph Rowntree Foundation, 1998).

Hunter, Caroline and Bretherton, Kerry, *Anti-social Behaviour. Law and Practice in Social Housing* (London, Lemos and Crane, 1998).

Introductory Tenancies Working Group, *Introductory Tenancies: Guidance for Local Authorities* (London, Local Government Association, undated).

Jensen, Lotte, ' Cultural Theory and Democratising Functional Domains: the Case of Danish Housing', *Public Administration*, 76:1 (1998), 117-139.

Karn, V., Lickiss, R., Hughes, D. and Crawley, J., *Neighbour Disputes: Responses by Social Landlords* (Coventry, Institute of Housing, 1993).

Keating, Peter, *Into Unknown England, 1886-1913* (Manchester, Manchester University Press, 1976).

Kelling, George and Coles, Catherine, *Fixing Broken Windows: Restoring Order and Reducing Crime in Our Communities* (New York, The Free Press, 1996).

Labour Party, *A Quiet Life: Tough Action on Criminal Neighbours* (London, Labour Party, 1995).

Lacey, Nicola and Zedner, Lucia, 'Community in German Criminal Justice: a Significant Absence?', *Social and Legal Studies*, 7.1 (March 1998), 7-25.

Lee, Peter and Murie, Alan, *Poverty, Housing Tenure and Social Exclusion* (Bristol, University of Bristol Policy Press, 1997).

Liddle, Mark, Warburton, Frank and Feloy, Mark, *Nuisance Problems in Brixton: Describing Local Experiences, Designing Effective Solutions* (London, NACRO, 1997).

Loader, Ian, Girling, Evi and Sparks, Richard, 'Narratives of Decline: Youth, Dis/order and Community in an English Middletown', *British Journal of Criminology*, 38:3, (Summer 1998), 388-403.

Local Government Ombudsman, *Annual Report, 1996/7* (London, The Commission for Local Administration in England, 1997).

Love, A. and Kirby, K., *Racial Incidents in Council Housing: the Local Authority Response* (London, Department of Environment, 1994).

Macey, John and Baker, Charles, *Housing Management*, 4th ed. (London, Estates Gazette, 1982).

Mackintosh, J. M., *Trends of Opinion about Public Health, 1901-51* (Oxford, Oxford University Press, 1953).

Malpass, Peter and Murie, Alan, *Housing Policy and Practice* (London, Macmillan, 1994).

Martin, C.R.A., *Slums and Slummers* (London, John Bale, Sons & Danielsson, 1935).

Matthews, Roger, 'Replacing "Broken Windows": Crime, Incivilities and Urban Change' in *Issues in Realist Criminology*, R. Matthews and J. Young (eds.) (London, Sage, 1992).

Maynard, W., *Witness Intimidation: Strategies for Prevention*, Police Research Group, Crime Prevention and Detection Series Paper 55 (London, Home Office, 1994).

Merry, Sally, *Urban Danger: Life in a Neighbourhood of Strangers* (Philadelphia, Temple University Press, 1981).

Morgan, James, *Safer Communities: the Local Delivery of Crime Prevention through the Partnership Approach*, Standing Conference on Crime Prevention (London, Home Office, 1991).

Morris, Sheridan, *Policing Problem Housing Estates,* Police Research Group, Crime Prevention and Detection Series Paper 74 (London, Home Office, 1996).

Murie, Alan, 'Linking Housing Changes to Crime', *Social Policy and Administration*, 31:5, (December 1997), 22-36.

— 'The Housing Divide' in *British Social Attitudes Survey* (Aldershot, Social and Community Planning Research, 1998).

National Association for the Care and Resettlement of Offenders (NACRO), *Crime, Community and Change: Taking Action on the Kingsmead Estate in Hackney* (London, NACRO, 1996).

National Society for Clean Air and Environmental Protection, *NSCA Noise Survey 1998* (Brighton, NSCA, 1998).

Neighbour Noise Working Party, *Review of the Effectiveness of Neighbour Noise Controls: Conclusions and Recommendations* (London, Department of Environment, Welsh Office and Scottish Office, 1995).

Newburn, Tim, Brown, David and Crisp, Debbie, 'Policing the Streets', *HORS Bulletin* 29 (London, Home Office, 1990), 10-17.

Newman, Oscar, *Defensible Space; People and Design in the Violent City* (London, Architectural Press, 1972).

Nixon, Judy, Hunter, Caroline and Shayer, Sigrid, *The Use of Legal Remedies by Social Landlords to Deal with Neighbour Nuisance* (Sheffield, Sheffield Hallam University Centre for Regional Social and Economic Research, 1999).

Ormerod, Paul, 'Stopping Crime Spreading', *New Economy,* 4.2 (1997), 83-88.

Osborn, Steve, 'Reflections on the Effectiveness of Estate Improvement Programmes', in T. Bennett (ed), *Preventing Crime and Disorder: Targeting Strategies and Responsibilities* (Cambridge, University of Cambridge Institute of Criminology, 1996).

Osborn, Steve and Shaftoe, Henry, *Safer Neighbourhoods?: Successes and Failures in Crime Prevention* (London, Safe Neighbourhoods Unit, 1995).

Page, David, *Building for Communities: A study of New Housing Association Estates* (York, Joseph Rowntree Foundation, 1993).

Painter, Kate, 'Different Worlds. The Spatial, Temporal and Social Dimensions of Female Victimisation', in D. Evans, N. Fyfe and D. Herbert, (eds), *Crime, Policing and Place* (London, Routledge, 1992).

Parker, H., Bakx, K. and Newcombe, R., *Living with Heroin: The Impact of a Drugs "Epidemic" on an English Community* (Milton Keynes, Open University, 1988).

Parker, Howard, Bury, Catherine and Egginton, Roy, *New Heroin Outbreaks Among Young People in England and Wales,* Police Research Group, Crime Prevention and Detection Series, Paper 92 (London, Home Office, 1998).

Pawson, Hal , 'Supply, But No demand', *Inside Housing,* 2 October 1998, 18-19.

Pearson, Geoffrey, *Hooligan: A History of Respectable Fears* (London, Macmillan, 1983).

Pearson, Geoffrey, 'Social Deprivation, Unemployment and Patterns of Heroin', in N. Dorn and N. South (eds), *A Land Fit for Heroin?: Drug Policies, Prevention and Practice* (Basingstoke, Macmillan, 1987).

Pearson, G., Blagg, H., Smith, D., Sampson, A., and Stubbs, P., 'Crime, Community and Conflict: The Multi-Agency Approach', in D. Downes (ed), *Unravelling Criminal Justice* (London, Macmillan, 1992).

Pitts, John and Hope, Tim, 'The Local Politics of Inclusion: The State and Community Safety', *Social Policy and Administration,* 31:5 (December 1997), 37-58.

Popplestone, Gerry and Paris, Chris, *Managing Difficult Tenants,* Centre for Environmental Studies Research Series 30 (London, CES, 1979).

Power, Anne, *Property Before People* (London, Allen and Unwin, 1987).

— 'Housing, Community and Crime' in D. Downes (ed), *Crime and the City, Essays in Memory of John Barron Mays* (Basingstoke, Macmillan, 1989).

— *Estates on the Edge: The Social Consequences of Mass Housing in Northern Europe* (Basingstoke, Macmillan, 1997).

Power, Anne and Mumford, Katherine, *The Slow Death of Great Cities? Urban Abandonment or Urban Renaissance* (York, Joseph Rowntree Foundation 1999).

Power, Anne and Tunstall, Rebecca, *Swimming Against the Tide: Polarisation or Progress on 20 Unpopular Housing Estates, 1980-1995* (York, Joseph Rowntree Foundation, 1995).

— *Dangerous Disorder: Riots and Violent Disturbances in 13 Areas of Britain, 1991-92* (York, Joseph Rowntree Foundation, 1997).

Ramsay, Malcolm and Spiller, Josephine, *Drug Misuse Declared in 1996: Latest Results from the British Crime Survey,* Home Office Research Study 172 (London, Home Office, 1997).

Reade, E.J., 'Residential Decay, Household Movement and Class Structure', *Policy and Politics,* 10:1 (1982), 27-45.

Reiner, Robert, 'Media Made Criminality', in M. Maguire, R. Morgan and R. Reiner (eds), *The Oxford Handbook of Criminology,* 2nd ed. (Oxford, Oxford University Press, 1997).

Report of the Committee on Housing in Greater London ('The Milner-Holland Report'), Cmd 2605 (London, HMSO, 1967).

Revolving Doors Agency, *Risk Factors in Tenancy Breakdown for People with Mental Health Problems* (London, RDA, 1997).

Reynolds, Frances, *The Problem Housing Estate* (Aldershot, Gower, 1986).

Ryder, Robert, 'Council house building in County Durham, 1900-39' in M. Daunton (ed), *Councillors and Tenants: Local Authority Housing in England and Wales, 1919-39* (Leicester, Leicester University Press, 1984).

Sampson, Alice and Phillips, Coretta, *Multiple Victimisation: Racial Attacks on an East London Estate,* Crime Prevention Series Paper 36 (London, Home Office, 1992).

— *Reducing Repeat Victimisation on an East London Estate,* Police Research Group, Crime Detection and Prevention Series Paper 67 (London, Home Office, 1995).

Sampson, R. and Laub, J., *Crime in the Making: Pathways and Turning Points Through Life* (Cambridge Mass., Havard University Press, 1993).

Scottish Affairs Committee, *Housing and Anti-Social Behaviour,* Parliamentary Papers, HC 160 1996/97 (London, Stationery Office, 1996).

Scottish Office Development Department, *Housing and Neighbour Problems: A Draft Circular* (Edinburgh, Scottish Office, March 1998).

Shapland, Joanna, 'Targeted Crime Reduction: The Needs of Local Groups', in T. Bennett (ed), *Preventing Crime and Disorder: Targeting Strategies and Responsibilities* (Cambridge, University of Cambridge Institute of Criminology, 1996).

Sherman, L. and Rogan, D., 'Deterrent Effects of Police Raids on Crack Houses : a Randomized, Controlled Experiment', *Justice Quarterly,* vol.12 (1995), 755-781.

Skogan, Wesley, 'Fear of Crime and Neighbourhood Change' in A. Reiss and M. Tonry (eds), *Communities and Crime. Crime and Justice: A Review of Research,* Vol. 8 (Chicago, University of Chicago Press, 1986).

— *Disorder and Decline* (New York, The Free Press, 1990).

Smith, Susan, 'News and the Dissemination of Fear', in J. Burgess and J. Gold, (eds), *Geography, The Media and Popular Culture* (Beckenham, Croom Helm, 1985).

Social Exclusion Unit, *Bringing People Together: A National Strategy for Neighbourhood Renewal* (London, Stationery Office, 1998).

Social Landlords Crime and Nuisance Group, *Anti-Social Behaviour in England, 1996/7: A Report on Patterns and Problems in Tackling Anti-social Neighbours* (Coventry, SLCNG, 1998).

Sumner, Colin, 'Rethinking Deviance', in Colin Sumner (ed), Censure, *Politics and Criminal Justice* (Milton Keynes, Open University Press, 1990).

'Taylor, Ian, 'Private Homes and Public Others', *British Journal of Criminology,* 35.2, (Spring 1995), 263-285.

Tebbutt, Kathy, 'Estate of the Nation', *The Big Issue,* June 22-28, 1998, 24-25.

Von Hirsch, Andrew and Wasik, Martin, 'Civil Disqualification Attending Conviction: A Suggested Conceptual Framework', *Cambridge Law Journal,* 56.3, (November 1997), 599-626.

Walklate, Sandra, ' "No More Excuses!": Young People, Victims and Making Amends', *Policy Studies*, 19:3/4, (December 1998), 213-222.

—'Crime and community: fear or trust?', *British Journal of Sociology*, 49:4 (December 1998), 550-569.

Walklate, Sandra and Evans, Karen 'Zero Tolerance or Community Tolerance? Policing and Community Talk about Crime in High Crime Areas', *Crime Prevention and Community Safety*, 1:1 (1999), 11-24.

Warburton, F., Liddle, M., and Smith, J., *Nuisance and Anti-Social Behaviour: A Report of a Survey of Local Authority Housing Departments*. (London, NACRO, 1998).

Wells, Celia, 'Stalking: The Criminal Law Response', *Criminal Law Review*, (1997), 463-470.

Wells, John, *Crime and Unemployment* (London, Employment Policy Institute, 1995)

White, Jerry, *The Worst Street in North London: Campbell Bunk, Islington, Between the Wars* (London, Routledge and Kegan Paul, 1986).

Wikström, Per-Olof, *Urban Crime, Criminals and Victims: The Swedish Experience in an Anglo-American Comparative Perspective* (New York, Springer Verlag, 1991).

—'Urban Neighbourhoods, Victimisation and Fear of Crime', in C. Fijnaut *et al* (eds) *Changes in Society, Crime and Criminal Justice*, Vol. 1. *Crime and Insecurity in the City*. (Antwerp, Kluwer Law International, 1995).

— 'Communities and Crime' in M. Tonry, (ed), *The Oxford Handbook of Crime and Punishment* (Oxford, Oxford University Press, 1998).

Wilson, Harriet, 'Parental Supervision: a Neglected Aspect of Delinquency', *British Journal of Criminology*, vol 20 (1980), 203-235.

Wilson, James Q. and Kelling, George, 'Broken Windows: the Police and Neighbourhood Safety', *The Atlantic Monthly*, March 1982, 29-37.

Wilson, William J., *The Truly Disadvantaged: The Inner City, the Underclass and Public Policy* (Chicago, University of Chicago Press, 1987).

—*When Work Disappears: The World of the New Urban Poor* (New York, Knopf, 1996)

Wohl, A.S., *The Eternal Slum: Housing and Social Policy in Victorian London* (London, E Arnold, 1977).

Women's Group for Public Welfare, Hygiene Group of, *Our Towns* (Oxford, WGPW, 1943).

Woolf, the Right Honourable Lord, Master of the Rolls, *Access to Justice: Final Report to the Lord Chancellor on the Civil Justice System in England and Wales* (London, HMSO, 1996).

Yelling, Jim, 'The Metropolitan Slum' in M. Gaskell (ed), *Slums* (Leicester, Leicester University Press, 1990).

Zedner, Lucia, 'In Pursuit of the Vernacular: Comparing Law and Order Discourse in Britain and Germany', *Social and Legal Studies*, 4:4 (December 1995), 517-534.

Index

Criminal Justice 2000: Strategies for a New Century
Michael Cavadino, Iain Crow and James Dignan
What is the nature of New Labour criminal justice policy? What strategic options does the government have for dealing with the problems of crime and punishment—and where is it likely to take us in future? This timely book analyses past and present policies in British criminal justice and distills a set of three broad options for its future, including a principled approach which seeks to protect the human rights of both offenders and victims by means such as rehabilitation, reintegration and restorative justice. 1999 ISBN Paperback 1 872 870 77 5. £20

Restoring Respect for Justice Martin Wright
This innovative work by Martin Wright takes his analysis of restorative justice to new heights—by way of an imaginative 'Symposium' of experts. Fully referenced and containing an analysis of developments since his acclaimed earlier work, *Justice for Victims and Offenders: A Restorative Response to Crime* (Waterside Press, 1996). 1999 ISBN 1 872 878 3. £18

Introduction to Criminology Russell Pond. A basic guide - written with people working in criminal in mind. 1999 ISBN 1 872 870 42 2. £13.50

Children Who Break the Law: or Everybody Does It Sarah Curtis
Chronicles at first hand young people talking about all aspects of their chaotic lives, their hopes for the future and their anxieties—where possible recording their parents views also. Sarah Curtis points out that *we do know* how to prevent much juvenile offending through community projects of proven benefit and other tried and tested means of reintegrating children in trouble with the law into schools, colleges, communities and careers. 1999 ISBN 1 872 870 76 7. £18

Introduction to Youth Justice
Winston Gordon, Philip Cuddy and Jonathan Black. Edited by Bryan Gibson
Deals with the major changes taking place in strategies for preventing youth crime and dealing with juveniles in and out of court, including the impact of the Crime and Disorder Act 1998, the creation of youth offending teams ('YOTs') and the responsibilities of local authorities and other agencies. Includes an authoritative and up-to-date outline of the youth court. 1999 ISBN 1 872 870 36 8 £13.50

Human Rights and the Courts: Bringing Justice Home
Edited by Bryan Gibson. 1999 ISBN 1 872 870 80 5. £10